CW00972362

Guildford Museum

Guildford Union Workhouse

Guildford

Uncovering the stories behind the facts

OUR TOWN

Guildford Castle

Guildford House Gallery

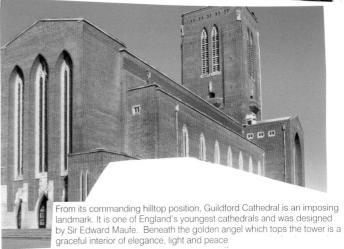

From its commanding hilltop position, Guildford Cathedral is an imposing landmark. It is one of England's youngest cathedrals and was designed by Sir Edward Maufe. Beneath the golden angel which tops the tower is a graceful interior of elegance, light and peace

Guildford Cathedral

Front endpaper
Guildford from the air in the days when the cattle market was off Woodbridge Road and the town had its own gasworks.

Back endpaper
Taken during the summer of 1975 when there were bus stations off Farnham Road and Onslow Street. The Friary Meux Brewery site has been cleared ready for redevelopment.

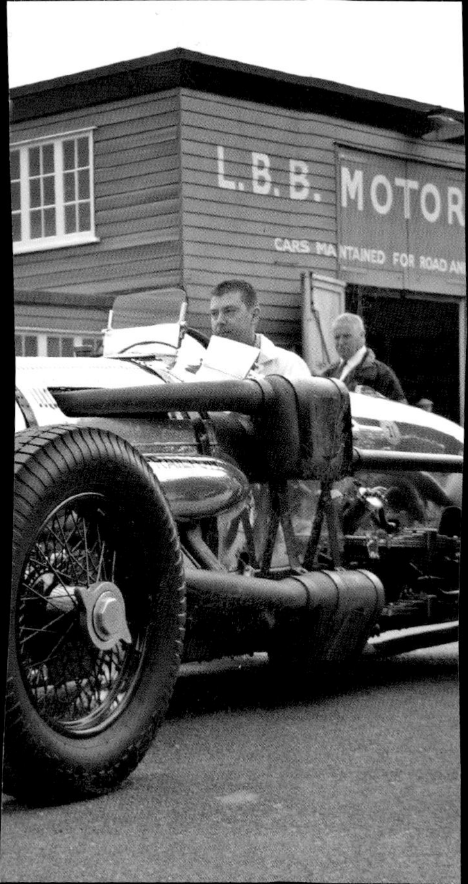
L.B.B. MOTOR
CARS MANTAINED FOR ROAD AN

Guildford
OUR TOWN

Uncovering the stories behind the facts

by David Rose

breedon **books**
PUBLISHING

First published in Great Britain in 2001 by
The Breedon Books Publishing Company Limited
Breedon House, 3 The Parker Centre, Derby, DE21 4SZ.

ISBN 1 85983 262 8

Printed and bound by Butler & Tanner, Frome,
Somerset, England.

Jacket printing by GreenShires, Leicester, England.

CONTENTS

Acknowledgments

The author wishes to thank the following who have contributed by way of lending photographs or who have passed on information and advice: Peter Bullen, Charles Brooking, Edna Chittleburgh, Graham Collyer and the *Surrey Advertiser*, Helen Davis of the Guildford Archaeological Society, Alan Davies, Dennis Vehicles, Ann Dent, Fred Emmings, Colin Fullagar (administrator of the Guildford Poyle Charities), the staff of Guildford Museum, Dennis Hammond, Norman Hamshere, Phil Harrington, Christopher Hilliard, Ray Jacques at the Guildhall, John Janaway, John Jones, Geoff Killick, Roger Majoribanks, Marion May, Eric Mills (archivist Guildford Cathedral), Bernard Parke, Susan Pink, David and Diane Peters, Steve Porter, Chris Quinn, Peter Quittenton, Joan Reid, George Riddle, Mike Searle, Mrs Searle, Andrea Selley of the National Trust Wey Navigations, the Shepard Archive at the University of Surrey, Frank Stokes, the Surrey Archaeological Society, John Sutton, John White, Clive Wicks, Dorothy Wright.

Thanks also to all the people I have spoken to or corresponded with regarding articles that have appeared in the *Surrey Advertiser*'s From the Archives column.

INTRODUCTION

MY fascination with Guildford and what has happened here over the centuries goes back a long way – to when I was a child. I clearly remember walking with my father along the trackway on The Mount and being told that it was a very old road. I was intrigued by this notion and could not help wondering what it would have looked like all those years before. I also wondered what the people were like who used it.

Another favourite walk was over Newlands Corner to the Silent Pool and hearing the story of the young girl who was bathing naked there when a dashing prince on horseback came upon her. Startled and afraid, she swam to a deeper part of the pool, lost her footing and drowned. Could this really have happened at this tranquil spot, I wondered?

As I learned more about the history of the town and heard other stories further questions came into my mind. For as long as I can remember, I have been intrigued to know how our forebears went about their daily lives.

I hanker to catch the feel of 1900s Guildford – the sound, the smells and the taste of it all. With a little imagination I find I can by just holding an old ginger beer bottle, the bowl of a clay tobacco pipe, or reading a message written on the back of an old picture postcard.

I have found another excellent way of actually stepping into the past; that is to read back copies of the town's local newspapers. I am fortunate that working for the *Surrey Advertiser*, I can actually touch and read those original copies which we have on file. The paper has usually yellowed and the copies are somewhat battered and a little brittle, yet by reading a month's worth of editions from any particular date I can guarantee that I have an instant all-round picture of what life was like then. It really is that simple.

I was particularly interested when books of vintage photographs began to be published in the late 1970s. These inspired me to begin my own collection of old picture postcards. Fortunately, thousands of views were published in the early years of the 20th century. Many were collected and cherished at the time and have survived to this day.

I have also enjoyed reading and collecting history books on Guildford and it is interesting to note how certain theories and accounts of events have changed over the last 100 years.

When my publisher, Breedon Books of Derby, inquired whether I would like to write a new book about Guildford I thought that the time was right to produce a book that records some of things which I believe are unique to this town. The book also includes some of the better-known stories about Guildford and its history and where possible brings them up to date.

Guildford Our Town, Uncovering the Stories Behind the Facts is therefore not a history of Guildford as such. It could be argued that in certain instances it also uncovers some of the facts behind the stories! And I have to admit that some of the subjects which I have chosen are ones that have had a particular interest to me at some point in my life.

However, I believe that anyone who has the slightest interest in the town's history, or who is just beginning to learn about it, will enjoy reading the following stories and looking at the collection of photographs and illustrations which I have provided.

Looking up the High Street with Abbot's Hospital on the left and the town decked out with flags and bunting to mark the coronation of George V on 22 June 1911.

HOW GUILDFORD
GOT ITS NAME

THE question is often asked how Guildford got its name. Does the town take its name from the golden sand that lines the bed of the River Wey? Or the yellow kingcups growing in the water meadows? Perhaps it has something to do with the Guild Merchants who governed the town in ancient times?

Currently, historians believe the first suggestion to be the correct answer. They say the name Guildford comes from the word Gyldeford – the golden ford – and dates back to the time of the first settlers in the early 500s. These Saxons would have lived in a small group of wooden huts, but exactly where, archaeology has yet to provide an answer. It may have been on the west bank of the river in the area around today's Portsmouth Road as they certainly had a burial ground at what is now Guildown. However, they could just have easily settled on the east side of the river where the first real town grew up.

Yet, until comparatively recently the Guild Merchant theory was still talked of. In a 1930s official guide to Guildford the then honorary remembrancer (or recorder

Bright yellow kingcups, also known as marsh marigolds (Caltha palustris), beside the River Wey near St Catherine's. A possible contender for the origin of the name – Guildford.

The golden sand at St Catherine's where it meets the River Wey. The site has been a crossing point of the river for centuries.

Edwardian view of the ferry crossing at St Catherine's.

of town events) Dr George Williamson, put the guild idea ahead of the golden sand suggestion, but added cautiously that the town must have had its origins long before any guild existed.

He suggested that the name was probably derived from the river, which, he went on to say, was once called the Gil, or Gilou. Williamson added that another suggestion gives the name of the river as the Wiley, and hence, Wey. On all of this he would not commit himself one hundred per cent.

Into the 1970s and in the book *Guildford a Biography*, by E.R. Chamberlin, we find the kingcups or marsh marigold theory holding sway. Russell Chamberlin chose this idea, but again was cautious to point out that 'there are few studies more full of traps than that of place-names'.

He added that some could still argue legitimately that the concept of 'golden' might be derived from the bright yellow sand that marks the crossing of the river.

But who is to say that another generation of writers

and historians will not come to a different conclusion? One thing we can be sure of is that history often has to be rewritten.

We do know that the earliest written evidence of Guildford dates back to the AD 880s when, in the will of Alfred the Great, a royal residence of his at 'Gyldeford' was left to his brother's son, Ethelwald.

Unfortunately, there is yet another story that claims Astolat was once the name of the town. The Victorians had a fascination with the medieval period and they may have contributed further by putting the name Astolat on the mythological map.

Written in the 15th-century, the book *Le Morte d'Arthur,* by Sir Thomas Malory, is a collection of tales about King Arthur and his Knights of the Round Table.

The author described how Sir Lancelot on his way to Camelot – set as Winchester in the book – stops for the night in a town which the author calls Astolat. He goes on to write 'now in English it is called Guildford'. Astolat may be a very old word and Guildford was certainly a

The inn sign at the Astolat public house in Old Palace Road.

place where people rested on their journey to Winchester. Perhaps there is a grain of truth in there somewhere.

However, Astolat gave rise to several businesses adopting the name, hence, the Astolat Tea Rooms that were once in the High Street near the Lion Hotel, the Astolat Garden Centre formerly at Peasmarsh and the Astolat pub in Old Palace Road on the edge of Onslow Village, that opened in 1961.

Furthermore, Malory wrote about a beautiful woman called Elaine, the 'Fair Maid of Astolat' whom Sir Lancelot fell in love with. And even British Railways may, unwittingly, have given credence to the myth when in the 1950s it named a number of steam locomotives from characters, places and objects who appeared in Arthurian legends. Along with *Merlin*, *Tintagel* and *Excalibur*, were those named *Maid of Astolat* and *Elaine*. Young trainspotters would have seen these passing through Guildford and may have asked questions about their origins. It's possible that the answers bandied about on the platforms at the station, like those around the bar of the Astolat pub, were 'something to do with Guildford in the olden times'.

GUILDOWN AND THE MASSACRE

WHEN a gardener discovered human remains in the grounds of a house in Guildown Avenue he could not have known that they would give credence to a 900-year-old tale of treachery

One of the pagan graves in the Saxon cemetery on Guildown. (Surrey Archaeological Society)

and mass murder – the darkest deed on record ever to have occurred in Guildford.

Whose Bones? ran the headline in the *Surrey Weekly Press* on Friday 23 August 1929. The story went on to say that two skeletons had been dug up in the garden adjoining Chalk Hill, Guildown Avenue, off the Portsmouth Road, by the gardener of the property which was owned by a Mr J.W. Kempster.

Police officers were called and after the coroner had been consulted, it was decided that as the bones were in an advance state of decay, they must have been buried many years ago, therefore a criminal investigation was not necessary.

However, archaeologists soon conducted their own investigations and found the remains of about 200 bodies buried in shallow graves. Some had their limbs tied together and others, who had obviously been savagely butchered, had their dismembered body parts carelessly scattered about.

Many were buried less than 18 inches below the surface of the chalky soil. There were, however, the remains of 36 bodies buried at a greater depth. With these were grave goods that included knives, spear heads, brooches, buckles and two beautiful coloured glass beakers. At the time of the first discoveries, before the archaeologists had carefully excavated the site and had scraped away at the layers of history with their trowels, there was much speculation as to the age of the skeletons.

Glass beakers from the Guildown Saxon cemetery. (Surrey Archaeological Society)

The *Surrey Weekly Press* suggested that as the spot was near the old coaching road they could have been the victims of highwaymen. Another theory was that they were militiamen from the Napoleonic Wars who were camped in the area. It was speculated that perhaps two of them had a duel to settle a personal difference and afterwards their bodies were hurriedly buried before the rest of the soldiers moved on. A gibbet was once near this spot, so another suggestion was that they were the bodies of malefactors executed there. All of these were just wild suggestions plucked out of thin air and none proved to be anywhere near the truth.

The excavations revealed that there were two separate burials at the site. The 36 bodies found at a deeper depth with their possessions were Anglo-Saxon pagans from the sixth century and they included men, women and children. Their graves were properly spaced and aligned. The Saxons believed that items buried with them would travel with the soul to the afterlife.

Of the second set of burials, lying barely a couple of feet under the soil, were a total of 222 skeletons literally thrown into their graves in a haphazard manner. As more and more bones were discovered it was evident to

the archaeologists that this was no conventional burial. These poor souls had been brutally murdered.

The story of a bloody massacre that had evidently taken place in Guildford in 1036 and recorded in history by the *Anglo-Saxon Chronicle* was fairly well known to historians by 1929. The noted writer Eric Parker had retold the story in his 1908 guidebook *Highways & Byways in Surrey*, adding: 'fortunately, nobody need believe the story'. We still cannot be one hundred per cent sure, but the finds at Guildown appear extremely similar to this ancient written reference to the town.

Other grave goods such as these pots were found at Guildown. (Surrey Archaeological Society)

Before he died in 1035, King Cnut had nominated his son Harthacnut (born to a common-law wife) to rule England. However, as Harthacnut was busy protecting his homeland in Denmark, his half-brother Harold Harefoot was put in charge. There was trouble brewing from the sons of the late Ethelred the Unready, King of England from 979 to 1016. Their mother, Emma, had married Cnut after Ethelred's death, but her two sons were exiled in France.

One of them, Alfred the Atheling, landed in Kent intent on making his way to Winchester to see his mother and perhaps complain about Harold Harefoot proclaiming himself King Harold I.

Alfred met the Earl of Wessex, an advisor to his mother, whom he did not fear. Each with their respective armies, they rode together on the journey to Winchester. At Guildford, where there was a royal residence, they stopped to rest. Following supper the two sets of travellers bedded down for the night, but only one group went to sleep.

The tale states that in the middle of the night the Earl's men sprung up and butchered up to 600 of Alfred's men. Alfred was captured, blinded and died of his injuries in prison at Ely.

The reasons are obscure why the Earl ordered his men to commit this heinous act. Perhaps the Earl was trying to strengthen Harold's claim to the throne. Was 600 an accurate count of those killed? It has been suggested that the bodies were taken some distance from the town to Guildown for burial. Burying them in a pagan cemetery may have been a deliberate insult to the dead.

Another theory is that those who were killed were captured in the town and then taken to the area of their burial and executed on site. Whatever happened we cannot be sure.

GUILDFORD BLUE

FOR many years Guildford had been been true blue – and not just in the political sense. By the 13th century the town had become extremely wealthy and was famous for its blue cloth, much of which was exported to the Continent.

The West Surrey woollen trade was, for a couple of hundred years, big business: It used wool from the sheep that grazed on the North Downs. The fleeces would be gathered into large square woolsacks and carried by horses to weavers working in the local villages. (The coat of arms of the borough of Guildford incorporates a woolsack, the symbol of the wool trade, on either side of an illustration of a castle.)

Often, the weaver and all his family would be

Racks Close, where the newly-dyed Guildford blue cloth was laid out to dry on wooden racks.

engaged in turning the fleece into cloth. The children combing it to straighten the fibres, their mother spinning it with the aid of a spindle. The father would then place it on his loom and weave it into a material known as kersey – which we would recognise today as a light blanket.

Woad grows between 18in and 3ft high and has yellow flowers in the summer.

The cloth would then be taken to towns such as Guildford or Godalming where it would be fulled (cleaned) to remove the natural grease, and then dyed.

The cloth would be washed in the River Wey and then placed in wooden tubs filled with water and fuller's earth, that had been dug near Redhill. It was then trodden until the fuller's earth absorbed any remaining animal grease. The process eventually became mechanised and one of England's earliest fulling mills was in operation in Guildford by 1251. These water-powered mills incorporated large wooden hammers that pummelled the wet cloth in wooden troughs.

The next step was to dye the cloth a rich deep blue using a plant called woad.

At one time woad was plentiful throughout the British Isles and it is said that when Julius Caesar invaded the natives were stained with it. However, it was in such demand that supplies were being exhausted and therefore by Saxon times it was also imported from Europe.

Woad leaves were picked and chopped up into a paste in a horse-driven mill. They were then rolled by hand into balls, each the size of a 'ferthing luv' (a farthing loaf). After being dried in the sun for about a

Replica garments using cloth similar to that which was once made in Guildford.

month the woad balls were crumbled into a powder, sprinkled with water and allowed to ferment – a term known as couching.

The mixture was then put into barrels and transported to the dyer.

Britain's wet summers did not produce ideal drying conditions for woad. The best woad on the London market in 1580 was from Toulouse, which was sold for 10 shillings per hundred weight.

At the dyehouse the process would have started with the dyer pouring boiling water on to the couched woad in a vat. Soon a pigment called indigo would separate from the woad. Bran, together with lime and wood ash would be added in order to achieve the correct alkalinity.

Fermentation lasted three days during which time the heated liquid was stirred continuously.

Finally, the wetted cloth would be lowered into the vat. When it was removed it slowly turned blue as the air oxidised the soluble indigo – it must have seemed like magic to those watching.

The blue cloth was hung out to dry on frames or racks, hence the name Racks Close which we know today. Here it would be inspected and brushed with teasels to raise the nap which would then be cut off with shears.

Although the wool trade made the town rich, with it came dishonesty. Some manufacturers deliberately stretched the cloth before it was dry. The unsuspecting buyer would get a shock when it was wetted again and shrank back to its original size.

For 300 years accusations of cloth stretching was levelled at the Surrey wool trade and it was one of the reasons for its eventual downfall.

It was certainly in the doldrums by the early 17th century when Archbishop George Abbot wrote to the Mayor of Guildford suggesting that the wool trade be revived in the town of his birth. He donated £100

Guildford's coat of arms incorporating two wool sacks.

annually to be distributed in the form of loans to poor tradespeople to help them set up in business again. A building called the Manufacture was erected near Abbot's Hospital for the rejuvenated cloth industry. It was a bold idea, but unfortunately failed.

The Manufacture still stands today in North Street near the library and is known as the Cloth Hall. The tower and upper portion of the building are of a later date, possibly when it was in use as George Abbot's School. There is, of course, still a connection with cloth, as the Cloth Hall is currently an Edinburgh Woollen Mill fabric and clothes store.

MEDIEVAL MERCHANTS

GUILDFORD has one of the best preserved 13th-century undercrofts in the UK and it looks much the same today as when it was used as a shop during the Middle Ages. This stone-vaulted basement has been described by English Heritage as the finest medieval building of its kind.

It is at 72-74 High Street below a fashion shop and leased by Guildford Borough Council, who spent £127,000 on its restoration in the 1980s.

It was constructed with its ceiling just above street level allowing for a window to be included which provided some natural light, while steps lead down to the entrance. At one time a wooden-framed merchant's house would have stood above the undercroft. There are, however, the remains of a staircase that would have led up to the house.

The chamber measures about 30ft x 19ft and excavations in 1979 revealed that the original street frontage would have been of chalk blocks dressed with flints.

Inside, two central pillars support the arched stone vaulting; ribs are supported around the walls by carved brackets known as corbels. They resemble grotesque faces, beasts and monsters.

As builders got to grips with restoring the undercroft to become Guildford's tourist information centre, they encountered a number of problems with moisture and humidity. The official opening was delayed for some months but it was finally declared open by the then Minister of Tourism, Lord Strathclyde, in June 1990.

Two years later it received a design award from The Guildford Society, but by 1994 its daily use as a tourist

The Undercroft is now fitted out as a medieval wine merchant's shop. There are also information panels on the town's history.

The Undercroft has a number of carved brackets known as corbels. They resemble grotesque faces, beasts and monsters.

information centre was putting a strain on the structure. Not only was it receiving 86,000 visitors a year, but also the heating, lighting and air-conditioning was drying out the mortar between the wall stones. It was obvious that it could not stand that degree of use, so the tourist information centre was moved to a building in Tunsgate.

The borough has now transformed the undercroft into a replica medieval wine merchant's shop complete with wooden casks, pottery and furniture. There is also a table marked out as a counting board on which metal tokens and coins would have been placed to make calculations. It is from this style of table that we get the word counter, as found in our shops today.

The Undercroft is open to the public for several hours each week.

There are traces of about six other undercrofts in the High Street all dating from the same period. Guildford was a wealthy town during medieval times, largely due to the woollen industry. The rich merchants of the town would have had these undercrofts built by their master masons. Towns and cities in the UK where other undercrofts have been found include Chester, Southampton, Winchelsea, and Stamford in Lincolnshire, whose surviving undercrofts are very similar to ours. These places would also have been involved in the medieval import and export trade.

The Crypt restaurant at the Angel Hotel is something of a misnomer. This room was indeed once an under-croft although major renovation work in the 1970s replaced the decayed chalk of the original with reconstituted stone.

Crypts are only found below churches and it is rumoured that in the 19th-century wall paintings of a religious nature were discovered there giving rise to the story that it may once have been a friary.

Historians have found it difficult to place a date on when an inn was established on the site of the Angel Hotel. But whatever building stood at ground level in the 1300s, it was not an inn.

The remains of another undercroft were found under 83 High Street, on the corner with Swan Lane, when building work was being carried out in 1993.

Although plainer in appearance, it is thought that it pre-dates the other two examples mentioned here. Its ceiling was found to slope to a central ridge and there were no pillars, nor evidence of a window.

A SYNAGOGUE IN THE HIGH STREET?

TV CREWS and journalists from around the world descended on Guildford in 1996 when local archaeologists revealed that they had discovered what appeared to be a medieval Jewish synagogue.

There may not have been a great deal to see to the casual onlooker, but news teams jostled to peer into a pillared 12th-century chamber below the fashion store Principals, in the High Street.

It had been fully exposed when building work was

Guildford Museum's Mary Alexander and John Boas excavate the remains of the chamber believed to have been the place where Guildford's medieval Jewish community worshipped.

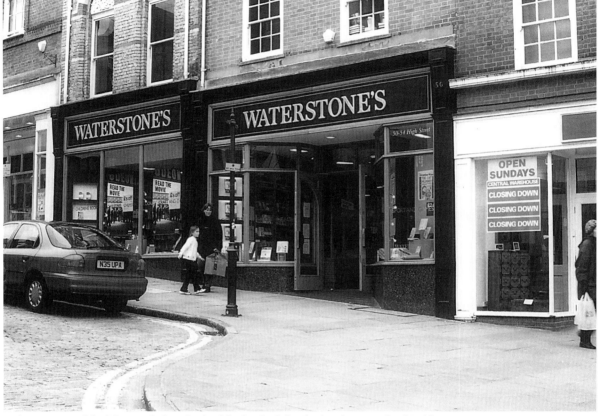

Today a Waterstone's bookshop stands above the site of the chamber believed to have been a medieval Jewish synagogue.

taking place and members of Guildford Museum's archaeological team were on site attempting to work out what the chamber once was.

A number of clues pointed to its use as a place of worship for Guildford's Jewish community during the 12th and 13th centuries.

When two shops in the High Street were being converted into one, the architects involved in the project asked Guildford Museum if there was any archaeology associated with the buildings. Some stone steps were a clue, so two holes were made in the wall of the cellar in one of the shops. Behind it was a chalk wall of a much older chamber. Fortunately, to make the conversion, a floor had to be lowered and this enabled the archaeologists to have a proper look at what they had discovered.

They found that the chamber had been well constructed with elaborate architecture. Mouldings on

a pilaster (a column attached to the face of a wall) resembled another in St Mary's Church in Quarry Street that dated from about 1160. Could the same masons have worked on both buildings? They were only a few hundred yards apart.

There were traces of wall paintings, which may have been imitations of tapestries or curtains. Samples of these were taken and the analysis revealed five different pigments had been used including indigo – the first time it had been found in English Romanesque wall paintings.

John Boas, of Guildford Museum, discovered scorch marks on a wall in a place where worshippers may have burned their eternal flame. Another significant clue to the chamber's use was the discovery of a silver coin deliberately wedged in the masonry where the Torah Scrolls would have been kept. (The first five books of the Bible, the early history of the Jews and many laws are written on the Torah Scrolls. Each scroll can be as long as 25 metres.)

Surviving tax records reveal that a prosperous Londoner, Issac of Southwark, had a house in Guildford, possibly the location of this chamber, and that it was attacked and looted by an armed gang in 1272.

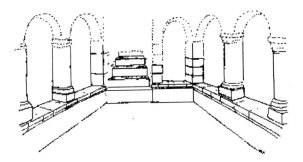

Drawing by Mary Alexander of how the room may have looked.

The profoundly religious Queen Eleanor, whose dower included Guildford Castle, expelled England's Jewish community in 1275. These facts tie in with the destruction of the chamber that the archaeologists found. They estimated that it had only lasted about 100 years. Medieval synagogues were often tall buildings. However, so as to conceal its real height, part of the building would have been constructed below ground.

At the time of the discovery, Britain's leading authority on English medieval Judaism, Joe Hillaby, of Bristol University, was convinced that all the evidence pointed to the chamber being a synagogue.

Its location was kept secret and only revealed after the shop's new occupants, the bookseller Dillons, had moved in.

Photographs of the floor of the chamber were taken and reproduced on parts of the new floor of the shop, along with several glass cabinets containing finds – many of these dating from later periods of history. They include shards of pottery, glass and clay tobacco pipes. Dillons is now a branch of Waterstone's bookshops but the artefacts are still on display.

One of the first visitors to the chamber was the leader of Guildford's Jewish community, Sid Cornbleet. He described the moment he stepped inside as very emotional, 'because', he said, 'the people who built it and prayed in it were not very different from ourselves'.

He added: 'If we came and joined in their services we would not notice any difference from our own, but there is no holiness left on this site, only sentimental associations.'

FRIARY TO FRIARY

FROM Dominican friary, to brewery and now today's shopping centre, the Friary site has had a long and eventful history.

When, in the early 1970s, the mainly Victorian Friary Brewery was pulled down, archaeologists had a field day excavating a site that revealed an important glimpse into a much older part of Guildford's history, hitherto unknown.

Eleanor of Provence, the widowed queen of Henry III, founded a friary in Guildford in 1274 in memory of her seven-year-old grandson, Prince Henry, who had died at Guildford Castle a few months earlier.

The Dominican or Black Friars were founded in Bologna in *c.* 1215-16 by St Dominic. The order spread throughout Europe and Asia. Its members did not seek solitude like other monks, but made their way to towns and preached to as many people as possible. Much of their income would have come from begging, although the Crown may have funded them from time to time.

The friary at Guildford was small compared to others in England with perhaps only 20 friars in residence at any one time. It contained a church with cloisters on either side which, in turn, was surrounded by domestic buildings.

It is reputed that the embalmed heart of young Prince Henry was kept in the church and put on public display each year on the anniversary of his death.

The archaeological digs of 1974 and 1978 led to a much greater understanding of Guildford's Dominican friary. The field officer and director of excavations was Robert Poulton. In an article in the *Surrey Advertiser* on 5 September 1978, he explained that he and his team had found an almost complete plan of the friary.

In its heyday it would have stood just outside the town as the medieval town ditch followed the line of today's North Street.

Mr Poulton said that excavations revealed a cemetery in an area between the friary's church and the town ditch. Sixty-five graves were excavated – 28 were in the nave of the church and the rest in the cemetery itself. It is believed that most of the burials would have been townsfolk as none of those excavated had any traces of grave goods, such as a chalice or a paten, which would have indicated that they were the priests' remains.

Five adults were found buried in one grave – possibly victims of the plague as suggested by Mr Poulton. In another grave were the bones of a mother and her child.

Those graves in the area of what would have been the church were better preserved. Here there were traces of wooden coffins suggesting that those laid to rest here would have been wealthier than those in the cemetery.

The Earl of Annadale, John Murray, built this mansion on the Friary site during the 17th century. It was pulled down in 1818.

Down she comes: a controlled explosion on Sunday 17 February 1974 demolishes the brewery tower.

The 'big hole' in the mid-1970s. Viewed from Onslow Street across to Commercial Road, this was where the Friary Meux brewery once stood.

There was, however, one lead coffin that contained the bones of a young woman, about 20 years old, buried in a shroud of fine linen. Mr Poulton concluded that she must have been a person of considerable wealth and importance.

There were many other finds that included a large number of bronze objects such as pins, strap ends, book studs and bootlace tags. Many of these were found in the area beneath what had been the choir stalls. Mr Poulton said that as the monks sat through the long services they were clearly unable to resist fiddling with anything to hand, and in consequence lost many small items.

The friary lasted until Henry VIII dissolved England's monasteries in 1538. It is recorded that by that time only eight friars were in residence and there was little opposition to its closure by them or by the people of the town.

Soon there were further developments on the site

which the Crown now owned. The church was pulled down and a house was built for Henry VIII. In the 17th century the Earl of Annadale, John Murray, acquired the site and built a mansion there which he called the Friary. The building stood until the early 19th century but had changed ownership, first passing into the hands of the Onslow family and then back to the Crown when, for several years, it became a barracks.

The mansion was demolished in 1818 and part of the land became a cricket pitch. It was also used as a public meeting placc and for circuses. In the 1840s its owners divided the area up and new developments appeared.

The Chennel family, who were bakers and millers, bought up a sizeable part of the former friary site and in 1858 Henry Chennel built a steam flour mill there. However, he died the following year aged 41, and the mill eventually passed into the ownership of the proprietor of the Cannon Brewery, Thomas Taunton.

It was he who founded the Friary Brewery using the

The Friary centre under construction in May 1980. Commercial Road and Woodbridge Road are to the right with the spire of St Saviour's Church clearly visible. The area where the crane is standing is now the bus station.

steam flour mill building. As it expanded more buildings were added. The chapter in this book on breweries and mineral water manufacturers gives further information about the history of the Friary Brewery.

A company of its size, with such a large number of employees both male and female, would certainly have produced many interesting tales of social history. Many will have been lost forever, but these two have been mentioned to the author.

The first concerns a man who worked in the boiler house and whose sweetheart worked in the bottling department. It is said that she used to smuggle out bottles of beer for him, which were then hidden in the

waste ash from the boilers. The brewery used a piece of waste ground opposite Stoke Mill where it dumped much of this waste ash as well as its old and broken bottles. Many years later, when the sliproad to the A3 bypass was being constructed, the road builders exposed the site. Some of the workers were surprised to find a large number of unopened bottles of Friary ale in the ash and cinders!

During World War Two there was a lookout post at the top of the brewery tower. It was the job of Don Moore, a junior clerk with Friary, to climb to the top of the tower if the air-raid siren sounded. His job was to keep watch for enemy aircraft.

At about lunchtime on 16 December 1942, he was

summoned to the look-out with its panoramic views of the town and shortly after heard two thumps as bombs exploded somewhere to the south of Guildford.

It was a German Dornier 217 aircraft that had attacked a train pulling out of Bramley railway station. Seven people lost their lives in the incident. It was not long before he saw the same aircraft heading towards Guildford. It flew quite close and he could clearly see its crew sitting in the cockpit. It then opened fired on the town with its machine-guns.

Other eye witnesses have suggested that the gunner was trying to aim for the railway station but was unable to fix his machine-gun at the right angle in relation to the aircraft's height. The bullets, however, rained over the old Royal Surrey County Hospital in Farnham Road and the County School opposite. Amazingly, no one was killed or injured, but the school still bears the scars with a couple of bullet holes still visible in the brickwork.

The 19th-century brewery tower has its own tale to tell. It was on Sunday 17 February 1974, when a controlled explosion raised it to the ground. The story goes that at the first attempt at about lunchtime the explosives failed to go off. The news that the tower was coming down quickly spread and by the time it was successfully brought down at 4.30pm crowds of onlookers had gathered around the Friary site in Onslow Street and along Bridge Street, to witness the spectacle.

The Friary centre was built by developers MEPC and was opened to the public as a shopping centre in November 1980. Its official opening, by Princess Alexandra, took place the following June.

A major refurbishment began in 1988 which created a lighter and more open-plan centre and the extremely short-lived Blackfriars public house (open for just seven years) became extra shop units.

But what became of the bones of the medieval skeletons found by the archaeologists? They had been removed to the Ancient Monuments laboratory in London where they were analysed by scientists.

They concluded that up to a third of the population of Guildford at that time would have died before they reached 30 years of age, although other inhabitants

Dust to dust. On 26 September 1987, the bones that had been excavated at the Friary site archaeological digs were reburied in St Mary's Churchyard. From left: The curator of Guildford Museum, Matthew Alexander, the Revd Dr Kenneth Stevenson, Bishop David Wilcox, and the Revd Stuart Thomas.

would have certainly lived to the ripe old age of 60. With the evidence they had before them, the scientists were unable to determine the sex of many of the skeletons. However, a great proportion appeared to have been male.

The teeth revealed much about the people of Guildford buried in the friary in the 13th century. They would have eaten a great deal of meat, but very little sugar. This assumption ties in with archaeologist Robert Poulton's theory that those buried in the church of the friary were wealthier than those whose last resting-place would have been in parish churchyards elsewhere in the town.

In September 1987 the curator of Guildford Museum, Matthew Alexander, told the *Surrey Advertiser* that it had always been the intention to re-bury the bones once they had been studied. And on Saturday 26 September that year, a service was held at St Mary's Church in Quarry Street and the bones were buried in the churchyard in a special wooden chest.

Permission to open the churchyard for this one-off burial had to be sought by an Order of Council which was granted by the Queen.

At the service, the then rector of Holy Trinity and St Mary's, the Revd Dr Kenneth Stevenson, said: 'It is a curious episode in the history of our town. Today, behind the pageantry of Guildford's medieval past, the spotlight has been on that chest.' He compared it with the uncertain journey that 'lies between Jesus and those who want to follow Him'.

GOING UNDERGROUND

STORIES are sometimes told of tunnels and caverns that run right under the town. It is even said that a tunnel once led from the castle under the River Wey and up to St Catherine's Hill.

Perhaps people are confusing them with a number of undercrofts that existed below buildings, such as today's Crypt restaurant at the Angel Hotel and the Undercroft itself. (See separate chapter.)

There are, however, caverns under part of the Castle Grounds. They form a number of chambers and passageways measuring 388ft from their entrance in Racks Close to their farthest point. For safety reasons, the entrance is now blocked up.

They were excavated during medieval times when the builders of the day required a particularly hard type of chalk, known as clunch. It occurs naturally several

A view inside the caverns.

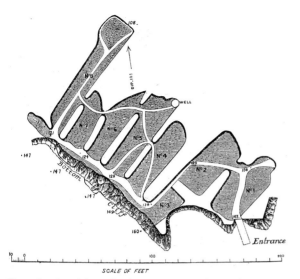

Illustrative plan of the Racks Close caverns. Note the site of a well.

feet down in the chalk on which parts of the town are built.

After the excavations had finished, the caverns were probably used as wine vaults and not, as has been suggested, a place of refuge if medieval Guildford was under the threat of an invasion.

Other suggestions have ranged from torture chambers (just as Racks Close was said to take its name from a certain instrument of torture) to once again hiding-places – this time for families who were fearful of William of Orange. The story goes that in 1688 rumours were spreading that a band of marauding Irish dragoons were coming. Perhaps some people hid inside the caverns, but the dragoons never showed up.

In the 19th century there was a prison on what is now Castle Hill and another unconfirmed story tells of a group of prisoners who, in 1831, were instructed to sink a well. In doing so they broke through to the caverns and thereby made their escape.

Before Racks Close became a public open space in 1911, the Guildford Rifle Club used it. In September 1905 it held a fund-raising event in which the whole of the grounds were lit with lanterns and fairy lights and the caverns were specially opened and guided tours were given. The *Surrey Advertiser* reported that the event had attracted 2,500 people. Gate receipts were £80, but the illuminated extravaganza had cost £40 to stage.

However, the organisers hailed the event a great success and the money raised would go towards improvements and an extension of the rifle range itself.

A huge Union Jack flag flanked by tall bamboo rods bearing Chinese lanterns hung at the entrance to Racks Close. Four thousand fairy lamps provided by Messers C.T. Brock & Co, were strung from trees and bushes.

The newspaper said 'strings of golden light were tastefully relieved by red and green, and all blended admirably, making one gorgeous whole'.

While the band of the 1st East Surrey Regiment played popular tunes, people formed a long queue and waited patiently to enter the caverns. The newspaper said that many people went down in the afternoon, but the rush in the evening was something of a revelation!

Fairy lamps, too, lighted the caverns, and the guides carried lanterns. Many of them were in fancy dress. One portrayed Merlin the Magician 'draped in long robes with wisdom locks and beard of grey, carrying in one hand a snake-like stick and in the other an old lantern, with *Old Moore's Almanac* thrust into his girdle'. Evidently, he 'kept his audience amused with his stories and humorous sallies'.

Other guides attempted to tell the history of the caverns. One story claimed that 600 Norman soldiers were massacred there. Many of the visitors were 'amazed at the way the flat roof (ceiling) had been hewn from the chalk'. The report noted the variation in height within the caverns – some places it being four feet and others seven feet. Visitors were forbidden from inscribing their

Glass fairy lights like these were used to illuminate the caverns and Racks Close during a fund-raising event in September 1905.

names on the caverns' walls, but were allowed to take a piece of chalk home as a memento. It also noted that the previous time the caverns had been opened to the public was in 1889.

The report ended by mentioning that a scent bottle had been found in the caverns during the evening and the owner could have it back on application to Mr A.E. Moon, Bank House, Guildford.

During World War One the caverns were investigated by the military as a possible place to store ammunition. However, an expert walked the dark passageways and soon came to the conclusion that they were far too damp to store explosives.

The caverns were opened to visitors once more between the wars. In 1930 they were lit by electricity and there were guided tours on Wednesday and Saturday afternoons or by appointment from the superintendent of the castle grounds. Entry was 6d for adults and 3d for children.

The Tearoom was a little shop in nearby Quarry Street, but by 1936 had changed its name to The Cavern.

No doubt the proprietors were hoping to attract some extra business from those that had just ventured into Guildford's dark dank underworld and were in need of a cuppa!

Dennis Hammond of Dorking was employed by the Guildford Corporation Electricity Works (later Seeboard) and rewired the electricity supply to the caverns. He says that the walls were so wet the wiring soon became faulty. It was also somewhat dangerous down there. He recalls the story about a caretaker switching off the lights one evening and receiving a nasty electric shock. In fact everything he touched appeared to be live!

With the outbreak of World War Two the tours of the caverns ceased and now they are considered too unsafe for visitors. They have, on occasions, been reopened when local building works have required some chalk clunch.

Anyone who did visit the caverns can consider themselves lucky. They are a part of Guildford that today's generation will almost never get to see.

ST CATHERINE'S FAIR

IN the 14th century an enterprising rector saw an opportunity to raise some money. He obtained a royal charter to hold a fair at St Catherine's Hill. It gave him the right to collect tolls and rents and the cash soon came rolling in.

It is recorded that on 4 November 1308, King Edward II granted the rector of St Nicolas, Richard Wauncey, whose parish the hill was in, the right to hold a fair on the site each year during the feast of St Matthew.

It was an ideal place at the busy crossroads of the trackway running east-west, following the line of the North Downs, and the route in and out of Guildford from the south.

Under the terms of the charter all inhabitants 'of the manor' were permitted to 'sell ale on payment of a small acknowledgement to the Lord', during the five-day fair.

However, the plucky rector did not have it all his own way. In 1318 the King took the rights of the fair away from him and handed them to the Rector of St Mary's Church.

Richard Wauncey had perhaps anticipated that he was in danger of losing his money-making venture. A year before he had the chapel on the top of St Catherine's Hill rebuilt, hoping it may strengthen his claim.

It may have been that he had other ideas of raising money and thought he could cash in on any pilgrims passing that way. It has been said that there were once two altars and placed in one of them a special relic or object to attract pilgrims. Perhaps these medieval 'tourists' were charged an extra fee to see it.

By 1328 the fair was back in the hands of St Nicolas parish, starting each year on 21 September. In pre-Christian times this had been the date of the autumn equinox festival, but the Church converted it to the feast of St Matthew. It also coincided with another local festival, the dedication of the church at Waverley Abbey, so there would have been plenty of people in the area.

In the early days the fair would have predominately sold food and ale for those travellers who were passing. Later it became a livestock market and then a general market with locally produced goods, including cloth, and pottery from nearby towns such as Farnham.

In 1563 the fair was cancelled due to an outbreak of

The ruins of the 13th-century chapel on top of St Catherine's Hill. It has sometimes been called Dragon Hill. It is said that the old name for the hill was Drake Hill. Drake being derived from draca – an Anglo-Saxon word meaning dragon. The connection between the hill and a dragon is unknown.

A view from the top of St Catherine's Hill looking towards the cottages in Ferry Lane. The house on the far right is The Beacon. When the railway tunnel collapsed in 1895 (see separate chapter) a summerhouse in the garden fell into a large hole created by the landslip. In 1975 The Beacon was demolished following a fire.

the plague. The date of fair was altered when, in 1752, the calendar was changed. Eleven days were added to the start date of St Catherine's Fair. Thereafter it began on 2 October each year.

There is a fascinating print of an engraving by J.H. Kernot of a watercolour painting of St Catherine's Fair by the famous artist J.M.W. Turner. The firm of Moon, Boys & Graves of Pall Mall, London published it, in 1832.

The canvas booths and stalls are pitched rather precariously up the steep hillside but there is much to see. At the bottom left clearly written on a booth is 'TRY the RED LION, NB not better under the SUN'. The Red Lion coaching inn stood on the corner of today's High Street and Market Street. And there have been several pubs in Guildford called the Sun. At about this time there was one in Quarry Street.

Halfway up the hill on the left can be seen Richardson's booth. He was a travelling showman from London. Further on people are taking rides in swing boats, and dotted about are several boys playing drums.

Staffordshire ware is on sale to the right from Baker the Crockman of Uxbridge, and slap bang in the middle of the road are a group of people watching a backsword bout.

Of English origin, the game was played with singlesticks. The first of the two contestants who drew blood from his opponent's head was pronounced the winner.

The Sunday before the fair began was known as Tap-Up Sunday when all the local people of St Catherine's village had the right to sell their home-brewed beer without a licence,

Tap-Up Sunday in 1863 ended up as a riot. While researching the Guildford Guy Riots, Gavin Morgan uncovered some interesting reports published in the national *Times* newspaper on 29 September of that year. It wrote: 'Upwards of 400 young fellows, many of them being low characters of Guildford, assembled in the village (St Catherine's) lining the road on either side; and when any peaceably inclined passenger approached they closed in and inflicted both insult and injury.'

The well-known print from an engraving by J.H. Kernot of J.M.W. Turner's watercolour painting of St Catherine's Fair, showing all the revelries in full swing. It dates from 1832.

The report added that about 30 people were seriously injured including a Mr and Mrs Piggott who were driving through the village and that 'Mrs Piggott had her bonnet torn from her head'.

Other women were 'rudely assaulted' and one had her eye cut from a stone that was hurled in her direction. Others had their 'hats smashed and coats torn to shreds'.

In the evening several policemen arrived on the scene but the newspaper said this was only the signal for more riotous demonstrations and it was considered advisable, for public safety, to leave the mob to their own course. The police, it would seem, backed off some distance and suggested that anyone using the Portsmouth Road that night should make a detour around St Catherine's village.

Finally, the rioters tore up the wooden railings in front of a house of a resident, who had pleaded for calm,

and burned them on a big bonfire near the railway cutting between the two tunnels.

No one, it would seem, was caught and prosecuted. However, the Home Office told the chief constable of the Surrey Constabulary that Acts of Parliament existed that overruled the ancient charter which allowed people to sell beer without a licence and that in future he must arrest anybody caught doing so.

By the early 20th century the fair was in rapid decline and the last fair held there was in 1914.

It was, however, revived for one year in 1984, when the then rector of St Nicolas, the Revd Brian Taylor, decided to exercise his right and hold a fair at St Catherine's – this time to raise money for the roof and organ appeal of St Nicolas Church. To give the fair some authenticity the curator of Guildford Museum, Matthew Alexander, staged a demonstration of backsword fighting, and thankfully there were no riots.

ADVENTURES OF THE CHAINED LIBRARY

T HE Royal Grammar School is home to one of Guildford's treasures – a chained library. During the many years that it has been at the school, it has, as pointed out by Mark Sturley in his book on the history of the school, had several 'adventures'.

Chained libraries date back to medieval times. In those days books were a rare commodity and they were chained to their bookcases simply because they were likely to be stolen.

Perhaps the most famous in the UK is the one at Hereford Cathedral which has volumes dating back to the eighth century. That collection totals some 1,500

The Royal Grammar School pictured in the 19th century.

The Bishop of Norwich, John Parkhurst, 1512-75, who bestowed a number of books from his collection and other gifts to Guildford.

books. According to the Library History Database, found on the internet, there are over 300 chained libraries in England.

The chained library at the Royal Grammar School is not so large as the one at Hereford, but is nevertheless very interesting. The books had once been in the collection of a Bishop of Norwich, John Parkhurst, who was born in 1512, of a Guildford family.

It is thought that he was first educated at Robert Beckingham's School in Guildford, the forerunner of the present Royal Grammar School. Parkhurst went on to Oxford and in about 1543 was appointed chaplain to Henry VIII's wife, Catherine Parr.

He fled England while the Catholic Queen Mary was on the throne returning after the accession of Elizabeth I. It was she who appointed him Bishop of Norwich in 1560. He died in 1575 and in his will he remembered his home town bestowing upon it several gifts. Included were his books that were not

written in English. His will stated that he left them 'to the Lybrarie of the same Towne ioyning the Schole.' He also gave Guildford a silver bowl, a basin and ewer, and 'I gyve to the poore of Guildford ffyve pounds'.

There was a delay in getting the books down from Norwich and it is said that the then Chancellor of the Exchequer had to intervene demanding that the books, the silverware and cash be handed over.

When the books finally arrived at the Royal Grammar School they were checked and listed. They numbered 87 volumes and were placed in a newly built gallery linking the Master's House and the Usher's House.

A former mayor of Guildford, George Austin, built the gallery that contains the chained library books in 1586.

Over the years books have been added to this historic library at the school and it now contains more than 480 volumes, some 90 of which are chained.

The oldest book is *Diomedes, De Arte Grammatica*, printed in Venice in 1480. Another interesting volume is one, which features the imprint of the great printer William Caxton. It is a copy of *Nova Legenda Angliae* by Capgrave, and was printed in 1516, not, unfortunately, by the 'father of the printing press' himself, but by his successor, Wynkyn de Worde.

With more books being added, the library was extended in 1648. However, by the 1840s, with the school facing economic difficulties, the library was dismantled.

Early 20th-century picture postcard view of the chained library. This room is now the office of the headmaster's secretary.

A committee was set up in 1863 to examine the books, some of which, by then, were in need of repair and restoration. The headmaster at the time and the Mayor of Guildford sat on this committee. It reported that the books should be reinstated at the school. It had been suggested that perhaps the books could form part of a public library. However, the committee responded by saying that although the books were of great historical significance, few citizens of the town would be interested in attempting to read them.

The books that required attention were transferred to Abbot's Hospital and the following year experts from London came to Guildford to value the books. Some (up to 96 it is believed) were removed and never seen again, while others that were found to be in a poor condition were simply thrown away.

However, the remaining books were not returned to the school's library for a number of years. Until 1897 they were stored in a warehouse belonging to the Guildford historian Dr George Williamson.

New bookcases were then added in a room within the part of the school known as the Usher's House and finally the books were reinstated.

As Mark Sturley points out, in 1941 the books were again on the move. This time they were removed for safe keeping to the crypt of the unfinished Guildford Cathedral along with other priceless items belonging to the borough, in case Hitler's Luftwaffe bombed the town.

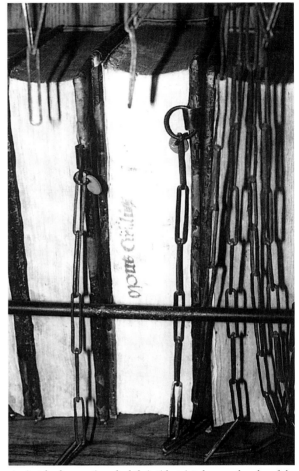

Ancient books sometimes had their title printed across the edge of the pages.

Happily, they were safely back at the Royal Grammar School after World War Two, but in 1953 were moved once again, this time within the school itself. A new school library was created and the books were transferred back to their original location on the first-floor gallery.

But the story does not end there. The fire that swept through the school in 1962 very nearly destroyed the historic books. Fortunately, they survived although some were blacked by the smoke of the fire and made wet by the water used to douse the flames. They were removed to Guildford library to dry out and were returned to the Royal Grammar School in 1965, when the building had been restored.

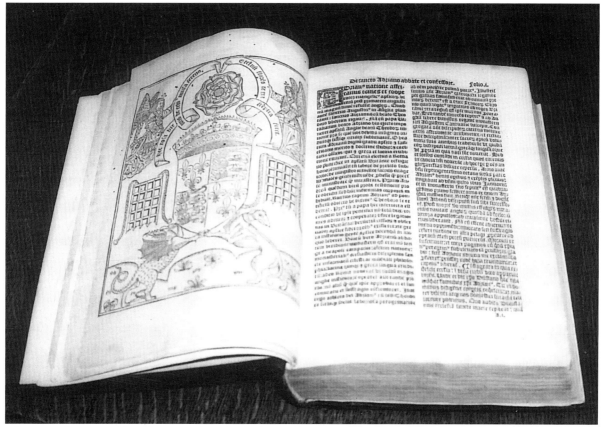

John Capgrave's Nova Legenda Anglie, c.1516. The earliest book in the library dates from 1475 and the latest is from 1858.

These days the books are still in the gallery – now the study of the school's headmaster, Tim Young. Certain volumes are restored as and when required. The books are read by scholars and historians and can be viewed by appointment through the headmaster's secretary, Barbara Wright.

She has a great knowledge of the library and often gives conducted tours of it when the school is open to the public each September on Heritage Open Day.

A GAME OF CRECKETT

THERE are many conflicting opinions regarding the origins of the game of cricket, but Guildford can lay claim to almost certainly having the first written account of it in Britain.

Cricket historians widely accept that the Greeks and the Romans were playing a game that involved throwing a ball at wooden stakes at least 2,000 years ago. Some say a game in which a bat was used originated in northern India and reached Europe via Persia in the eighth century. Others claim that it had reached these shores by the time of the Norman Conquest of 1066.

It is said that the first certain reference to 'criquet' is contained in a document dated December 1487 at a place called St Olmer. Sorry to say, it's not in Britain, but an area thought to be north-west France!

The word itself produces plenty of conflicting theories. Criquet to the Flemish or Dutch was a piece of furniture on which one kneels in church. Criccee to Anglo-Saxons was 'crooked staff' or a piece of wood with a club at one end.

Taking these ideas further, it's reckoned that cricket developed from a game called club-ball in which a person with a bat defended a hole in the ground. There are plenty of religious connections, including the fact that games similar to cricket were played in church-yards.

There are those who say the game was first played by shepherds using their crooks to defend the wicket gate of their sheep folds from a stone or even a pine cone thrown by an opposing player.

However, we will probably never know in what shape or form the game had developed when it was being played in Guildford in the 16th century. It would be pleasing to think, however, that it was similar to today's game.

How it may have looked. In 1998 cricketer Darren Bicknell dressed up in Tudor clothing and was photographed at the top of North Street on the site believed to have been where cricket was played in the 16th century. This occasion, however, was to mark the 60th anniversary of professional cricket in Guildford. The first county match was between Surrey and Hampshire in 1938. Darren and his brother Martin were born in Ash and graduated through Guildford Cricket Club's colts system, both going on to play for Surrey. Darren is currently with Nottinghamshire.

There exists the minutes of a lawsuit heard in 1596 before the 'Guildford Curia legalis' relating to a case of unlawful enclosure of a piece of wasteland in the parish of Holy Trinity.

The court heard that the land in question had lately been used as a garden and that an 'innholder' by the name of John Parvish, who by the time of the trial had died, had also laid claim to it. Representing the Crown was a Surrey coroner by the name of John Derrick, aged 59.

He told the court that he knew this piece of land well and that for many years it had been used 'by the inhabitants of Guldeford' as an area to saw timber and make wooden frames. He added that he had been a scholar at the Royal Grammar School and said: 'Hee and his fellowes did runne and play there at Creckett and other plaies'. He added that this piece of land had also been used for the baiting of bears!

So where did John Derrick and his school friends enjoy what is still our national summer game? It is thought that the piece of land in question was at the top of today's North Street, probably where the building now occupied by the restaurant TGI Friday's and County Sound Radio, stands.

The court document was put on show in 1948 by The Guildford Society and the writer and naturalist Eric Parker, who lived at Hambledon, took a great interest in it. An ardent cricket fan, a few years later he published his meticulously-researched book *History of Cricket.*

In the book Eric Parker writes that after the Guildford reference to the game, no others can be found relating to Surrey for another 100 years. The first recorded match, according to some historians, took place in Sussex in 1697.

Perhaps John Derrick and his cricketing friends were lucky to get away with playing their games as during the previous century pastimes such as these were often banned. Adults caught playing such pursuits could be heavily fined especially if they were neglecting their archery practice!

You may still hear people say 'cricket was first played in Guildford'. This probably arises from references to it which often appeared in town guidebooks some 30 to 40 years ago. We do have an early written reference to the game in Britain, perhaps the first, but it was surely being played elsewhere at the same time.

THE ARCHBISHOP'S LEGACY

FROM humble beginnings as the son of a Guildford cloth worker, George Abbot rose to become Archbishop of Canterbury. He is the town's most significant figure within the nation's history and has been described as Guildford's Godfather.

He may not have been the best archbishop Britain has known, taking up his position at a time of turmoil in the Church of England, but in his later life he did not forsake his home town and its people. He gifted it an almshouse of which he said was 'out of my love to the place of my birth'.

George Abbot was born in 1562 in a small cottage that stood not far from the public house, which today bears his name opposite St Nicolas Church. A story is told that his mother, when pregnant, dreamed that if she were to eat a pike the child she gave birth to would become famous. Not long after she drew a bucket of water from the River Wey and in it was a small pike. It was duly cooked and eaten.

The story became known locally and when old enough, three wealthy godparents paid for young George to attend the Royal Grammar School. He excelled at his studies and at the age of 16 went to Balliol College, Oxford, from where he graduated at the age of 20.

However, he was not the only member of his family to make a name for himself. One of his five brothers became Bishop of Salisbury, another was a Lord Mayor of London and another a Mayor of Guildford.

Entering holy orders, George remained at Oxford

Archbishop George Abbot (1562-1633).

and in 1597 became master of University College. Three years later he became Dean of Winchester.

He was one of 54 revisers who translated a new version of the Bible that was published in 1611 which is

The ornate tomb of Archbishop George Abbot in Holy Trinity Church.

Archbishop George Abbot's statue at the top of Guildford High Street.

known today as the Authorised Version or Kings James' Bible. That same year James I appointed him Archbishop of Canterbury.

His was a difficult time to be archbishop as there were deep divisions in the Church. He eventually lost the support of James when he refused to approve the divorce of the Earl of Essex and Lady Francis Howard.

A tragic event that was to cast a shadow over the rest of his life occurred in the summer of 1621. His friend, Lord Zouche had invited the archbishop, to take a holiday with him at his house near Bramshill in north Hampshire. Following the consecration of a new chapel, the archbishop joined a hunting party. He was by no means an expert with a crossbow and shot Peter Hawkins, a gamekeeper, in the arm, who then bled to death.

His enemies at once demanded that taking a man's life, albeit accidental, should result in him being removed from his position as primate of the Church of England.

James I, however, pardoned him from any guilt, but it was a bitter blow to the archbishop who became increasingly unwell and retired from public life to his palace near Croydon, where he died in 1633.

The appearance of the Hospital of the Blessed Trinity which stands in the High Street has changed little since George Abbot saw this, his gift to the town, built. He laid its foundation stone in 1619 and the building was completed within two years. Built of locally made brick, it is somewhat reminiscent of Oxford or Cambridge colleges. It is one of the best examples of Tudor brickwork in the South of England, although when constructed its style was going out of fashion.

Abbot's Hospital, seen here in about 1900, is one of the best examples of Tudor brickwork in the South of England.

Commonly known as Abbot's Hospital, it has never treated the sick, but was built for, and still is, a home for the elderly. George Abbot stipulated that the hospital should have a master and 12 'brothers' and eight 'sisters', all of whom were to be unmarried, over the age of 60 and either born in Guildford, or had resided in the town for 20 years.

The occupants, he said, were to wear blue caps and gowns (in remembrance of Guildford blue cloth) and a silver badge in the shape of an archbishop's mitre.

It was his intention that it would be a community, rather than separate homes. Those allowed to live there were people who had held prominent positions in the town or who had run businesses, or those men who had been in the services. The archbishop chose them personally following advice from friends and relatives in the town.

The chapel was central to daily life and there were four feasts a year. Residents were encouraged to find some kind of suitable employment, but not the keeping of an alehouse! They were allowed to leave the hospital for short periods, craftwork was encouraged, but begging was strictly forbidden.

By the early years of the 20th century the formal gowns were only worn in chapel. Nowadays it is only the master who wears one on ceremonial occasions.

By the 1970s it was realised that to meet modern standards as a home for the elderly further accommodation was necessary. This posed a problem of how to add a sympathetic extension to arguably Guildford's most beautiful building. It also stood in a conservation area. An inquiry took place and in December 1979 the Environment Secretary granted the governors of Abbot's Hospital permission to extend the building.

Twelve flats were built on land that had been part of

Turn of the 20th-century view of the Quadrangle within Abbot's Hospital.

the hospital's garden adjoining North Street. The design, to complement the existing buildings, was by the architects Nye Saunders & Partners. The work was completed in March 1984 when there was a topping out ceremony with the master, Gerard Taylor, laying the final tile on the roof.

The design and placing of statues often causes much debate and Guildford's statue of Archbishop George Abbot is no exception.

Cast in bronze and standing nine feet high on a plinth of Cornish granite and Portland stone, it cost £32,500 and was unveiled in 1993 by the then Archbishop of Canterbury, Dr Robert Runcie.

But while sculptor Faith Winter of Puttenham worked on the larger than life image, there was plenty of talk over who was going to pay for it. Some Guildford councillors thought the money would be better spent on more needy projects in the borough, others hoped that the statute would be a good investment and would benefit tourism.

Faith Winter had said: 'Sculpturally, this is a marvellous way to depict him with the added grace of his ecclesiastical garments. I really do believe the sculpture will enhance Guildford.'

In February 1992, it was decided that the money for the statue would be raised by public subscription and contributions from developers. A businessman from Aldershot, John Hine, then stepped in offering to help raise the cash. The council agreed and announced that two town centre developers were now contributing to environmental improvements in exchange for the borough relaxing outdated planning rules. So, £15,000 from Baker Tilley and £5,000 from Premier Investment Management Services was transferred to the statue fund.

By August 1992 a further £800 had been raised. The unveiling ceremony took place in April 1993.

Lord Runcie said: 'This splendid statue presents us with a strong man but at the same time gentle, and I think this is a faithful picture of the preacher and kindly

Looking down to the Quadrangle with residents wearing the traditional caps and gowns.

Th extension is finished. The Master of Abbot's Hospital, Gerard Taylor, lays the final tile on the roof at the topping out ceremony on 11 March 1984. Pictured with him is the site foreman Tim Jenkins (left), and the architect of the project, Richard Greening.

pastor that he was.' However, after its unveiling the statue still hit the local newspaper headlines with comments from critics and plaudits alike.

In October 1993, sculptor Faith Winter was presented with the William Crabtree Memorial Award for outstanding contribution to civic design, by The Guildford Society. But a letter writer to the *Surrey Advertiser* was astonished that the statue should earn a special award at all as he thought, compared to modern statues he had recently seen in Denmark and Norway, it was 'heavy, static, monolithic and dull – and furthermore, an error was made in placing such a bulk in such a confined space'.

He did go on to make the point though of suggesting that if the 'civic fathers' were now looking for local icons, why not adopt rock guitarist Eric Clapton or entertainer Harry Secombe?

Building work is in progress on the extension to Abbot's Hospital in 1983.

MAKING THE GUILDHALL CLOCK TICK

THE symbol of Guildford is its famous Guildhall and the clock that projects over the High Street. But how many people realise that the mechanism is not within its gilded case but inside the roof-space of the hall itself?

The mechanism is a series of interlocking cog wheels, two pulleys on which are wound the steel cables that work the clock and bell machinery, and a large weight that plunges to the bottom of the building. Connected to the clock mechanism is a rod that in turn is connected to dials on the clock face outside. Originally, ropes were used before the steel cables replaced them.

The clock is wound three times a week – Mondays, Wednesdays and Fridays. Access to the loft is through a door on the first floor. It leads to a tiny space where

Christopher Hilliard of jewellers Mappin & Webb has the task of winding up the clock three times a week.

directly in front is a steel ladder, bolted to the wall. At the top is a small platform and a door that leads to a dark loft full of exposed beams and centuries of dust.

The rarely-seen mechanism of the Guildhall clock housed in the roof of the Guildhall.

Switch on a light and about 30 feet away in the gloom is a raised rough wooden box in which the clock mechanism is housed. Wooden boards lead to it and you can hear its rhythmic ticking as you approach. Open the door of the box and the wonderful cogs and metalwork are revealed.

Chalked on one side of the box are the words 'please wind slowly', a gentle reminder of this historic and quite beautiful piece of equipment.

Russell Chamberlin in his book, *Guildford A Biography* (Macmillan & Co Ltd, 1970), described the

The Guildhall and the clock are the symbol of Guildford. This early 20th-century view was published as a postcard by the photographer Percy Lloyd of Albury.

In the roof space of the Guildhall are two glass clock dials, placed neatly on top of one another. They were used for a period towards the end of the 19th century.

Close-up of the bell that strikes out the hours across Guildford High Street.

The bell in place today was presented to the town in 1931 by councillor W.R. Philpot. Here the previous one, that had cracked, is removed. It is now on view in the entrance of the Guildhall.

mechanism as remarkably simple, almost skeletal in appearance. Few, who have had the privilege to see it and hear it ticking away, would disagree with him.

The Guildhall itself has its origins as being the meeting place of the town's Guild Merchant, a body of tradespeople who, from medieval times, ruled the town for several hundred years. A 14th-century Guildhall once stood on the site, but the hall of the Guildhall, now forming the middle part, dates from 1589. The elegant frontage and the bell tower were added in 1683.

The Guildhall has also served as a court for municipal rulings and to hear criminal cases. In 1934 a new portion was added to the back of the building as a retiring room for judges and magistrates. Substantial refurbishment took place in 1986 that included the installation of a new heating system and alterations to the entrance hall and kitchen. The interior wood panelling was cleaned, the outside repainted and the clock regilded.

It is not often that one is able to see the view from the bell tower on top of the Guildhall. While photographing the clock mechanism, Surrey Advertiser *photographer Steve Porter also had the opportunity to take this photograph.*

could not afford to pay the Guild Merchant the required fee, or was refused, so he made a clock and presented it to the town.

No one knows the truth of the story and when it was supposed to have occurred. A John Aylward was given the freedom of the borough in 1684 and it is believed that it is only the clock case which dates from 1683, as clearly painted on it. The mechanism seems to predate it – perhaps by more than 100 years.

It has been suggested that there may have been two Aylwards, or perhaps if the 17th century Aylward did indeed present a clock to the town, did he incorporate into it parts that were much older? Some of its parts have been replaced over the years as they have become worn. John Smith & Son of Derby currently service it. Occasionally a more thorough examination is carried out at which time passers by may have looked up and been surprised to see the main part of the dial missing.

In the late 19th century these dials could have been lost forever when they were removed and replaced by glass dials lit by gas lamps. They were about to be sold for scrap when their importance was realised and the glass taken out and the original dials reinstated.

Today, those glass dials rest gently against a beam inside the Guildhall roof-space, and it is noticeable that one or two visitors have written their initials in the layers of dust covering them.

On 23 October 1940, the borough council took the decision to remove the clock case for safekeeping for the duration of World War Two. Its hiding place was not revealed but it is now generally acknowledged as

The original bell, reputedly from St Martha's Church near Chilworth, cracked and was replaced in 1931. It now stands in the entrance hall.

The age of the clock, however, has puzzled historians for many years. The story goes that a clockmaker from London called John Aylward came to Guildford seeking permission to set up in business in the town. Either he being the crypt of the then partly-built Guildford Cathedral.

In place of the clock were two large discs attached to the supporting beam over the High Street. The one facing east was printed with a wartime message: LEND TO DEFEND OUR FREEDOM. HELP ME TO SAVE MY FACE.

Not long after peace had been declared, Guildford's much-loved clock was returned to the Guildhall and received a well-earned overhaul by the staff of jewellers Salisbury & Son, who had been associated with its maintenance for generations. It was put back in its rightful place on 6 September 1945.

Today, Christopher Hilliard of the jewellers Mappin & Webb looks after it. He has been 'winder-in-chief' for over six years, and was previously understudy to Keith Gates who worked for the jewellers Salisbury's.

He is therefore well used to climbing the ladder to delicately wind up the clock. He says the reason that it must be wound slowly is to ensure that the cables do not jump off the pulleys. Evidently, it is quite a job getting them back on again.

On the day the author met him he was also helping the Guildhall's custodian, Ray Jacques, take down a flag from the mast projecting from the bell tower.

When the start of British Summertime comes around Mr Hilliard gets up early on the Sunday morning and puts the clock forward an hour. With the end of British Summertime he stops the clock for one hour on the Saturday night. To do this he has to shut the bell off. He says people regularly count the strikes and if they notice that something appears to be wrong, he's soon told!

He added that considering its age the clock mechanism is in remarkable condition. He admitted that it does gain a bit of time and every so often he has to stop it for a couple of minutes. I wonder if anyone notices?

DICING FOR THE MAID'S MONEY

DICING for the Maid's Money is a unique contest that has taken place in Guildford for more than 300 years. But maids (or domestic servants) who live under the same roof as their employers appear to be in decline, so it's getting harder attracting contestants.

In his will, dated 27 January 1674, Guildfordian John How left £400 to be invested and after several years an amount awarded annually to a poor maid who had served with good character. Contestants were to throw dice or cast lots to determine who should receive the money. His actual words were: 'The maid which throweth most on the said dice at the throw, or to whom the lot falleth.'

The first payout is recorded as being in 1687 and it is thought that How died in about 1676. He did not want his money squandered and in his will he placed certain restrictions on the choice of maid. They had to be of good report and had to have served their master or mistress for two years. They must not, he stated, live at an inn, alehouse or tavern.

It is also rumoured that the idea was to start the recipient off with her 'bottom drawer' or money to help set her up for married life. A loser in the contest was to be allowed to take part for a further two years.

In 1728 How's money was invested in South Sea Annuities and the interest paid to the Mayor of Guildford for distribution.

The 2001 Dicing for the Maid's Money contest was held at the Guildhall on 10 May. Here Antonia Chittenden scores 10 with her two dice, making her the winner. However, Dorothy Hobbs, who is looking on, and who scored seven, took home the greater amount of money. She received a cheque for £62, while Antonia received £60.

The wooden box, made by students at Guildford College, containing items associated with the Dicing for the Maid's Money. David Williamson, a past chairman, presented the chairman's gavel to the trustees in 1901. The shaker is made of hide with a silver base and rim. The dice are kept in a beautiful snuff box presented by Harry Savage, another past trustee. The wording on the lid reads: 'This was purchased in Guildford. Keep in Remembrance of that delightful place. The Beauty of Surrey.'

Another charity was set up by John Parsons for impoverished male apprentices in the borough, but if the money was not claimed it could be paid to the maid who had thrown the lowest score on the dice when competing for How's charity money.

As John Parsons had left a larger amount of money to be invested, it means that the loser of the dice contest ends up richer – but only by a few pounds!

The last male claimant to Parsons' charity was an apprentice cabinetmaker named Albert Russell in 1909.

At the 2001 dicing, held at the Guildhall on 10 May, the contestants were Antonia Chittenden, and Dorothy Hobbs, both employed by the Guildford Association of Voluntary Services.

The dicing was over in the blink of an eye. Antonia scored 10, beating Dorothy's seven. And so, as always, the winner ended up the loser. Antonia collected £60 from How's charity while Dorothy took home a cheque for £62 from Parsons' charity.

It is interesting to compare the amounts paid out over the years as the original account books still exist. Between 1706-38 Parsons' charity paid out £30 each year. From 1796 to 1824 it paid out £21 5s 6d annually. The records show that in 1796 How's charity was paying £10 15s. In 1893, Parsons' paid out £13 7s 10d, while How's paid £12 12s.

Today, the two charities and the Dicing for the Maid's Money contest is run by the Guildford Poyle Charities.

One of the ledger books that have recorded the Dicing for the Maid's Money down the centuries.

In 1984 to meet inflation it boosted the funds of How's and Parsons' charities from other charities that it administers. These include the Poyle Charity itself, which is the largest. The philanthropist Henry Smith started this in the 17th century following a gift of £1,000 to Guildford.

He was a wealthy London jeweller, but quite eccentric. It is said that he visited towns and villages dressed as a beggar. Later he bequeathed money to those places that had treated him well. To those that had put him in the stocks and ridiculed him, he left nothing.

The Guildford Poyle Charities is managed by 18 trustees and in 2000 received 276 applications for assistance. It paid out a total of £28,578 in lump sum grants.

Applications are from social workers, health visitors and community mental health teams. There are also requests for assistance for disabled people and those who are in need of shoes, clothing, electric appliances and other household items.

The administrator of the Guildford Poyle Charities is Colin Fullagar. He admits that he is finding it harder to attract contestants for the dicing, despite appeals in the local press. The criteria for entrants has now been changed slightly, so the 'maids' no longer have to live in with their employers. They don't have to be a spinster either! However, it was decided that they must have been employed by their employer for at least two years and the employer must reside in the borough of Guildford.

The dicing takes place at the annual meeting of the Guildford Poyle Charities, and in 1993 an oak box, inlaid with sycamore, laburnum, yew and plane – all Guildford-grown wood, was presented to the charities' clerk William Norris. Students at Guildford College made it and in it is kept the Maid's Money dice, shaker and the chairman's gavel.

LIFE ON THE WEY NAVIGATION

THE Wey Navigation from the Thames at Weybridge to Guildford has a unique place in history. This stretch of the River Wey can lay claim to some of the first pound locks in Britain and was one of the first to be canalised. The Stevens family were connected with it for nearly 150 years; they kept it going as a commercial waterway even though its traditional cargoes were slowly being transferred to the railways and onto the roads.

The first people to alter the course of the River Wey

The preserved barge Reliance *can be visited at Dapdune Wharf. She was built between May 1931 and June 1932 and worked between Guildford and the London docks. Eventually sold in 1969, she was found in 1989 abandoned on the mudflats at Leigh-on-Sea in Essex. The barge was refloated, towed back to Guildford and refurbished in 1995.*

William Stevens I (1777-1856).

help of the Earl of Arundel he received a commission from Charles I in 1635 to proceed with a survey of the river and to carry out the work. The plan was delayed by the Civil War, but afterwards, on 26 June 1651, an Act of Parliament was granted to 'Guildford Corporation and others to make the Wey navigable at their own expense'. The town's business community was hoping the navigation would help bring some prosperity back to the town after the collapse of the woollen and cloth industry.

Williams Stevens II (1810-90).

were millers, who by the 13th century had cut artificial channels to divert water to their mills. Farmers, too, began damming river channels to flood winter pastures creating a warmer and more fertile soil to produce lush grass for their dairy cattle the following spring.

Sir Richard Weston, of Sutton Place, was born in 1591 and educated in Flanders. He was impressed at the way pound locks were used in the Low Countries to control the flow of water and make rivers navigable. He was particularly interested in ways to improve agriculture and so in the 1630s he built a pound lock at Stoke. He then constructed a channel about 5km long known as the Flowing River that enabled him to control the water around the meadows of his estate, thus flooding them when necessary.

His next idea was to make the River Wey navigable from the Thames at Weybridge to Guildford. With the

Sir Richard enlisted the help of James Pitson, a former major in Oliver Cromwell's army, to construct the waterway. Pitson raised capital and negotiated with landowners through whose land it was to be built. He'd been instrumental by using his influence with Cromwell to get the Act itself through Parliament.

Richard Scotcher, from Guildford, was another important person in its construction. Pitson made him foreman and treasurer of the project, but he ended up in prison over debts that mounted up. While serving his sentence he wrote an essay entitled *The Origins of the Wey Navigation* in which he pointed a finger at Pitson for certain financial irregularities and dealings.

The navigation was one of the first inland waterways in Britain and was completed in just two years. It comprised nine miles of canal, with 12 locks and 20 bridges. About 200 men were employed in its construction. They included the navvies who dug 'the cut', blacksmiths, carpenters, masons and turfers. Although it cost only £16,000 (about £1 million today) the project ran up huge debts.

Scotcher recorded these and it seems that a large number of employees and suppliers had not been paid.

Sir Richard Weston died in May 1652 and did not live to see his waterway completed, but his family felt the backlash of the scheme – they were left with the all the debts.

Pitson persuaded one of Sir Richard's sons, George Weston, to act as foreman and provide further financial support. He too was soon in financial difficulties, was sent to prison and forced to sell his family's remaining shares in the project. Pitson, who then had almost total control of the waterway, snapped these up. The Weston family received no profits at all from the scheme.

Even when the waterway was opened in 1653 and ready for business the financial situation still dragged on. The canal's water level became dangerously low following several dry years with the result that laden barges were unable to move. Scotcher, however, still had to dig deep into his own pocket to pay the bargemen's wages.

A commission was appointed to investigate the running of the navigation and sort out the problems. However, the situation did not really improve until the monarchy was restored in 1660 and Charles II came to the throne.

A second Act with regard to the Wey Navigation was passed in 1661 and handed control to six trustees. By this time Richard Scotcher was dead, but James Pitson went on to become a justice of the peace and a county commissioner. He also spent some time in prison, but retired to Leapale House in Stoke-next-Guildford and died there on 1 May 1692.

Slowly the navigation prospered and so did Guildford as barge traffic increased taking agricultural produce, flour, paper, wooden items and even beer, to London. By the 1720s it carried an average of 17,000 tons of produce per year, generating about £2,000 worth of revenue by its tolls. This had risen to £5,860 by 1800, when it carried 57,500 tons.

The association of the Stevens family and the navigation goes back four generations to William Stevens I (1777-1856), who was a carpenter by trade. In 1812 he became the Triggs Lock keeper, between Sutton Place and Send. He had married Harriet Chandler whose father, Stephen, was the master carpenter on the navigation. It was he who most likely fixed William up with the lock keeper's job.

In 1822 he secured the important job as lock keeper at Thames Lock, Weybridge, where he learned to make accurate records of the cargoes being transported on the waterway. Three years later he became wharfinger at Guildford. Here he raised his family of three sons and two daughters, Sadly, his wife died in 1825, giving birth to twins.

His eldest son, also named William (1810-90), became a carpenter and by 1840 had built his own barge, *Perseverance*, and was trading on the navigation.

Evidently, William I did not approve of his son's bid to enter the barge trade, considering it a risky business. However, the gamble paid off and by 1847, William II had a new barge *Reliance*, and by 1857 owned three more and had seven men working for him.

He had been employed part-time by his father as assistant wharfinger at Guildford and after his father had died, took up the position full-time.

He too named his first son William (1844-1936), and like his father and grandfather before him he too trained as a carpenter, and with his brother John, joined their father's business.

Trading as William Stevens & Sons, by the 1890s it had a fleet of eight barges and a monopoly of the navigation.

William Stevens III (1844-1936).

A barge is launched sideways into the River Wey at Dapdune Wharf. In 1894, William Stevens III employed Edwin Edwards, who had been a master carpenter on the Kennet & Avon Canal in Wiltshire. With his wife and six children they moved into a cottage at Dapdune Wharf. The Surrey Advertiser of 27 October 1909, reported the launching of a new barge. It said that it had been built of best Sussex oak by George Edwards, aged 26; A. Edwards, 22; E. Edwards, 16; and A. Edwards, 14.

An opportunity had arisen in 1889 to buy more shares in the Wey Navigation. Although William II was wary, the two sons went ahead and made the purchase. Finally, in 1902, they gained overall financial ownership and the majority of the tolls.

By this time the company was flourishing and also ran a coal merchants business and undertook maritime civil engineering as well as having steam tugs on the River Thames.

The fourth generation of Stevens to work the navigation was William III's son, Harry (1887-1970). He took over the running of the business in 1929 and in 1964 transferred ownership of the navigation to the National Trust in order that the waterway be preserved. The last commercial load was carried in July 1969.

The National Trust acquired the Godalming Navigation (from Millmead in Guildford to the wharf at Godalming) from its commissioners in 1968. Today the

The navigation offices off Friary Street were demolished in the 1970s.

Harry Stevens (1887-1970).

National Trust looks after the 20-mile stretch of waterway from Godalming to Weybridge, calling it the Wey Navigations. Its headquarters is at Dapdune Wharf in Guildford, where Stevens' barges were constructed and overhauled. There is a visitor centre which gives a fascinating insight into the history of the navigations. The National Trust strives to protect the navigation from possible intrusive development near to its course and to preserving wildlife. It also monitors the pressures put on the waterway caused by increased recreational use and the decline in farming.

The National Trust at Dapdune Wharf has also built up an important archive of historical photographs and information. In 1989-90 Desmond Briscoe recorded some of those who had worked on the Wey Navigation in the first half of the 20th century as they recalled their memories.

Ernie Edgar with one of Stevens' horses at Guildford wharf.

The late Ben Haslett was a barge skipper for six years but as boy had cadged rides on the boats when his uncle worked for William Stevens & Sons. In 1947, when he was about 13½, he was offered a job as a cabin boy by another skipper by the name of George Fisher. Ben's mother was not at all amused when her son came home to tell her that he'd been offered work, but against her advice, and the fact that his father was away in the Army, he'd made up his mind and got his way.

When interviewed by Desmond Briscoe he said life was very hard for a young boy on the barges. Unlike the narrow boats of the Midland canals, these barges were not powered by engines while on the Wey Navigation, but either pulled by horse or by hand. In cold weather he said the ropes were like barbed wire.

The barges would ply their trade between the London docks and corn mills such as Coxes near Send and Bowyer's at Stoke. Wheat from Canada was loaded into the Wey barges moored at either Victoria or Surrey Docks in the East End of London. The loading usually took place at night and when fully laden the crew (often just the skipper and his mate) would row the barge out of the dock to where they would moor up again, this time to a buoy, until daybreak. A tug would then tow the barge, in convoy with perhaps six others, up the Thames to Kingston or Brentford.

Another tug would then tow the Wey barge to Thames Lock at Weybridge where the crew would wait overnight before embarking on the journey back along the Wey Navigation. Ben said that the living accommodation was in the aft end of the barge. It was quite cramped with an old-fashioned range, a primus stove and a wireless that was powered by accumulator batteries.

Another of his jobs was to cook the skipper's meals and he recalled that many of the boatmen enjoyed a drink or two. Most skippers would supply his mate with food, but the fuel for the stove had to be scrounged from coal barges at the docks. It wasn't uncommon to pinch vegetables from allotments near the waterside and at Pyrford there lived a couple of tramps that always had cheap vegetables and eggs for sale. You didn't ask where they'd got them!

Sutton Place near Guildford, was the home of the Weston family.

Seen on board the Speedwell *at Thames Lock, Weybridge, in 1963, are, from left, Fred Glover, Capt Steve White (the barge's skipper) and Tony Harmsworth. John White followed in the footsteps of his father and also worked on the Wey barges. The Harmsworths were another well-known family who also had close connections with the Basingstoke Canal.*

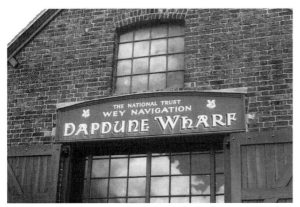

Dapdune Wharf is open to the public and tells the story of the Wey Navigations.

Although the men did not get paid holidays, the horses enjoyed two weeks each year on a farm near Triggs Lock.

He recalled his proudest moment as the time when Harry Stevens called him into his office and said he could take over as skipper of a recently refurbished barge. That evening he went down his local pub, the Bell, and celebrated with 'all the old fellows'.

Other families who once worked on the Wey Navigation he recalled as the Edwards, Groves, Leggs, Christmases, Gaffs and Fishers.

Until he got married he lived on the barges virtually

Other cargoes carried included timber, as far as Moon's at Guildford, and sulphur that was loaded at Shalford. It had come from Cranleigh and was taken by barge to London.

It was important not to let rainwater saturate the wheat. Although the barges had thick tarpaulin, it did sometimes get wet and could be refused by the miller. Soiled wheat would end up as animal feed.

Ben said that the pairs of horses used to pull the barges knew every inch of the towpath. They knew when to stop at the approach to locks and when to go slow or fast. Never were two new horses paired together, always one with an older horse until it had learned the lie of the towpath, which it usually did within a few weeks.

George Fisher inside a Wey barge.

Fred Legg aboard the Wey barge Hope. *The Fishers and Leggs were well-known Guildford families who worked on the Wey Navigations.*

Stoke Lock in the 19th century shows just how remote some of the countryside was for the men on the barges.

all of the time, only going home for a few days' rest and for a change of clothes.

Peter Fletcher grew up in Shalford and as a boy learned to swim, and to row and pole boats. In his teens in the 1940s he converted an old 24ft lifeboat, put an engine in it and sought permission from Harry Stevens to use it on the navigation.

When interviewed by Desmond Briscoe he said that it was forbidden to moor on the towpath side as horse-drawn barges could be on the river any time of the day or night.

Eventually, he got a job with Stevens and recalls the old-fashioned wharf buildings in Friary Street. Harry

Stoke Mill, seen here in about 1910, was built by the Bowyer family in 1879. Flour was milled for the last time in 1957 and it then became a paint factory/warehouse. It is now the offices of Surrey & Berkshire Newspapers Ltd, which includes the Surrey Advertiser *among its titles.*

Stevens sat in his office on the ground floor, which was below the level of Friary Street. It was a dark room with a low ceiling and was filled with sales ledgers and old documents. There was a fireplace in one corner, where Mr Stevens sat, and in the opposite corner a desk where the company secretary, Bill Smart, sat.

But Harry did not spend all his time stuck in his office. Peter said that once a week he cycled the whole length of the towpath to see what was going on along his beloved waterway.

THE TREADWHEEL CRANE

IDDEN inside a timber shelter beside the River Wey near the Town Bridge is probably the oldest treadwheel crane in Britain still in working order.

On the outside is the crane's main beam and jib that faces out over the river. Cargo was attached to an iron hook at the end of a length of chain that was wound around a drum attached to the treadwheel. Men walking inside it powered this. A maximum load of three tons

Today the jib of the crane is in stark contrast with the modern buildings on the opposite side of the River Wey.

The treadwheel crane building in its original position in 1970 before this part of the waterfront and Friary Street were redeveloped.

could be lifted in and out of the barges moored beside it.

The crane (sometimes referred to as a treadmill crane) is now a scheduled ancient monument, but owing to a lack of documentation, it is not known exactly when it was built.

Experts have suggested that it may date from about the 1660s, soon after the town wharf was established. However, there is no mention of it in an inventory of 1676, while outhouses, wharf houses and sheds are listed on the same site.

The earliest reference seems to be in 1764, when crane rope costing £3 11s 6d was purchased, and it is first mentioned by name in a canal survey of 1826.

It once fitted snugly within the jumble of wharf buildings on one side of the river and those of Crooke's Brewery on the other. Today it looks and feels somewhat out of place amid the concrete and paving slabs of the town's river frontage and the roar of the traffic passing by on the gyratory system.

It now stands alone and not in its original position, although close to it. It was moved when Friary Street was redeveloped in the early 1970s.

Not all parts of the crane are original and it is likely that it has been rebuilt on at least three occasions. It is estimated that the wooden shelter was at some point completely replaced. The roof was renewed in the 19th century and the wheel itself modernised by the addition of steel bearings. Additional restoration and alterations took place when it was moved to its current position.

It is thought that it was last officially used in 1906, although it was still maintained by employees working for the Stevens family for many years thereafter.

OYEZ, OYEZ!

FOUR generations of the Peters family have cried out for the sake of Guildford, but luckily some of the more unusual and brutal duties once undertaken by the town crier and beadle have not been expected of them.

Today's duties, which add a touch of colour to ceremonial occasions while also promoting the heritage and history of the town, contrast with tasks that once included administering public whippings.

Writing in the *Surrey Times* in April 1952 on the history of the Guildford's beadle, or town crier, Mrs J.K. Green said that the last public whipping took place in 1830. It was ordered by the Mayor, William Elkins, who was henceforth known as Billy Whip, an indication of the growth of public opinion against such a spectacle. She writes: 'The prisoner was manacled by the wrist to the tail of a cart and dragged from the Angel Hotel to the Red Lion (on the corner of High Street and Market Street), being flogged by the then town crier, Timothy Lovett.'

Guildford's town crier for the last 12 years has been David Peters, who has followed in the footsteps of his father Arthur (town crier 1966-89), his grandfather Jessie (1946-66), and his great grandfather Albany (1911-46).

He says that when the public whippings took place the speed at which the town crier made the cart go depended on the amount of money the poor unfortunate victim could afford. If he were wealthy, it wouldn't take long for the cart to complete its journey!

In olden times the beadle was responsible to some extent for guarding the town (and the mayor). He made his nightly rounds crying out the state of the weather and the hour, ending his call with the words 'and all's well'.

An enactment in 1547 said that every parish should appoint a beadle who had the right to enter ale houses on Sundays and other Holy days at the time of divine service and fine all the people found drinking and eating, 6d. The beadle was allowed to keep 2d of each fine while the rest was paid to the mayor who was supposed to distribute it to the poor. It was both a means of paying the beadle and finding out who had not been attending church, or which masters were not ensuring that their servants or employees were at church!

George Cook was beadle from 1732-42 and records show that in 1742 the mayor had to pay a man called Harris 2s 6d for whipping Nathaniel Lintott, as Cook had either refused or quit his job. In the same year, and shortly before he was appointed beadle, John Apark received a tidy sum of £4 4s for whipping Richard Martin and Thomas Brooks.

The job of beadle also ran in the Apark family. There were three generations of them: John (1742-90, 1791-93), William (1793-1820), and James (1845-63). John's term of office was interrupted for a year when the night watchman, James Stephens, was also beadle. Timothy Lovett (1820-45) stepped in between William and James Apark, for 25 years.

One of John Apark's announcements in 1765 was to cry against allowing hogs, sows or pigs to go in public streets and passages, on pain of a fine of 6d. This was a paltry amount and very often no deterrent at all to the animals' owners who turned them out to feed among the refuse left by market traders.

William Apark is referred to in local records as beadle and town crier. Some of his tasks included the 'crying down' of things such as counterfeit money, gambling or illegal billposting. For each cry he received one shilling on top of his £2 a year salary and £2 for cleaning the Market House. However, he boosted his income further by being appointed the town's weigher of hay and straw, and measurer of wood.

Town crier Timothy Lovett had the unfortunate job of posting bills warning the town against the disease cholera, and crying 'mad dogs on the loose!' He also acted as a human advertiser for Stevens the fishmonger, doing what in TV and radio commercials today is called a voice over. J.K. Green told the story how Lovett went around with his bell crying: 'O yes! A large quantity of fine fresh herrings just arrived at Stevens. Twelve for a shilling. God save the King.'

The third and final Apark, James, was a trader of many different kinds of goods from his premises at 82 High Street, which was next to the Town Bridge. From there he sold fishing tackle and bait, including live minnows and gudgeons. He also sold 'aromatic cheroots' and 'scented fusees' and hired out boats. Another business interest of his was an 'original wholesale and retail ginger beer manufactory'.

James Harrison held the post of town crier from 1863-93, and W. Tilbury from 1893-1911. The 14lb bell used to gain attention from the crowds was then passed into the hands of the Peters family. Albany Peters originally used this bell, engraved with the names and dates of Lovett, Apark and Harrison. He was presented with a new bell, known as the Family Bell, for his services to the town during World War One. This is slightly smaller and lighter.

His great-grandson, David, actually uses another bell, a bargain buy for £20 from a second-hand shop!

He says that handbells should always look tarnished.

They are tuned to certain musical notes and should not be cleaned and polished in fear of them losing their correct tone.

The uniform he and his forebears have worn is from a style that was established during the early years of the 19th century. The design of the trim on his red cape with its gold banding is thought to be unique. He wears a black coat with red cuffs. Unlike many other town criers who wear knee breeches, the Guildford crier has for many years worn trousers. David Peters tends to wear a jabot around his neck, although his father and grandfather often wore bow ties. The trim on his tricorn hat is real oak-leaf gold.

His great-grandfather 'cried' at many public occasions including accompanying the mayor in a recruiting campaign for the Queen's Regiment at the outbreak of World War One.

Jessie Peters acted as deputy town crier taking over in his own right just before Albany died. His first 'cry' was in 1936 when he proclaimed the succession to the

Albany Peters (town crier and beadle 1911-46) leans out of a carriage window believed to have been when the first electric train arrived at Guildford via the Cobham line in 1925.

Guildford town crier Arthur Peters (1966-89) raises the decibels to promote a concert featuring the choirboys of Holy Trinity Church in 1982.

throne of Edward VIII. At one time Jessie was Surrey's only town crier and was a well-known musician playing saxophone, trumpet or drums in local jazz bands. In 1952 he formed the Guildford Sea Cadet Band and was the first person to train buglers at Brookwood War Cemetery for the playing of *Last Post* and *Reveille*, at special occasions.

The third of the Peters to don the town crier's cloak and hat was Arthur. Like his grandfather and father before him, he entered many town crier competitions travelling as far as Halifax, Nova Scotia in Canada. In 1982 he went to Bermuda with hundreds of other town criers from around the world for an international competition.

He too played in a number of bands and sang with the Surrey Fringe Barbershop Group and was a member of the choir at St John the Evangelist Church, Merrow.

David Peters, like his father, is a member of the Ancient and Honourable Guild of Town Criers. These

Albany Peter's duties were not confined to the borough of Guildford. The occasion and date is unknown but it would appear to be at the Pepperpot in Godalming.

Classic photograph of Arthur Peters outside the Guildhall. He worked for British Telecom and once featured on the cover of an edition of the Guildford area telephone book.

David Peters soon after he had taken over as Guildford's town crier and beadle in 1990.

days his duties are split between official ones and those which could be described as private functions or events.

Official duties include being present as beadle at the annual meeting of the council and the mayor making, when the new mayor is sworn in each May. The following Sunday there is usually a service for the new mayor at Holy Trinity Church and the beadle leads the procession from the Guildhall to the church and back again after the service.

Each October, when the judges begin their new circuit, there is a service for them at Holy Trinity. And again the beadle can be seen in attendance. He's back in the town yet again the following month for the Remembrance Day service.

David admits that the profile of the town crier and beadle is not so high as it once was. But as long as his cry is loud and clear, hopefully there will be a place for him in our town.

SEMAPHORE TOWERS

ONE of the highest points in Guildford is Semaphore House on Pewley Hill – a reminder of a communication link between the Admiralty in London and the naval fleet in Portsmouth, long before the telephone had been invented.

Defending Britain's coastline from invasion had been an important undertaking for centuries. Far better to repel an invader at sea rather than after it had landed,

and for those keeping watch it was vital to be able to pass messages quickly to and from headquarters and between naval bases.

The lighting of fires and beacons were the earliest means of raising the alarm, and during the French wars of the 18th century the Admiralty devised various signalling systems along the south coast using flags by day and lamps at night. The biggest problem was getting

An early 20th-century view that includes the house on Pewley Hill built as a semaphore tower.

The house as it looks today.

messages to and from Admiralty headquarters at Whitehall and Portsmouth, some 70 miles apart. It could take up to seven hours for a man on horseback to cover the distance which was dangerously slow, so a system was devised that used a chain of hilltop stations to signal one another.

The shutter telegraph was the invention of the Revd Lord George Murray. His system, which the Admiralty adopted in 1795, used a wooden hut on which was mounted a 20-foot framework, in which six wooden shutters were hung. With men on the ground using ropes a total of 63 different combinations of open and closed shutters could be formed, each spelling out numbers and letters. An observer with a telescope at the next station along the line would note the message and have it arranged on his framework which could then be read by the next station. The system worked well, unless rain or fog reduced visibility. The line extended from

London to Putney Heath, to Oxshott, through to Netley Heath near Gomshall, on to Hascombe Hill, then to Blackdown near Hindhead and so on to Portsmouth.

The shutter system was abandoned at the end of the French Wars in 1816. However, it was not long before the Admiralty realised that it had been a useful form of communication and decided to build a more permanent system and this time Guildford was on the route.

Thomas Goddard, a master mariner in navigation and signalling, was chosen to survey large parts of South East England to find the best sites for the new semaphore system, an invention of Rear Admiral Sir Home Popham.

Goddard tramped up hill and down through some of the area's most wooded and inhospitable countryside in his search for possible sites. He concluded that the previous route was not suitable, so he looked at other

This illustration shows the tower that once stood at Worplesdon near St Mary's Church. The tower was the first semaphore station on a proposed branch to Plymouth. It was pulled down in 1851.

locations. Finally, in February 1820, Goddard presented his recommendation to the Admiralty.

The Navy's top brass chose a route that required 15 semaphore stations to be built of brick with living accommodation for the operators. Most were fairly high towers to ensure the signalling equipment stood out above any obstacles in the vicinity, such as trees. The line itself followed the old shutter line out of London, but diverged at Putney Heath. There were stations at Kingston Hill, Telegraph Hill near Claygate, Chatley Heath near Ockham, Pewley Hill at Guildford, Bannicle Hill at Witley, Haste Hill at Haslemere and a further six stations in Hampshire on route to Portsmouth.

The equipment for the system consisted of a 30ft mast, with two 8ft long arms or signals that could be rotated into numerous positions by means of chains connected to a gear mechanism to spell out 48 separate characters and numbers. It was known as the Popham Vocabulary Code.

The buildings and towers varied in shape and size. For example, Pewley Hill station was built with three stories. The station at Cooper's Hill was a three-storey square tower house, but the one at Chatley Heath was constructed as a large five-storey octagonal tower. The termini stations at London and Portsmouth had a staff of three, but at the intermediate ones there was usually just an officer and one assistant – perhaps an old seaman who acted as lookout.

The system was up and running by 1822 and on a clear day a message could be sent from one end to the other in about 20 minutes. Three years later a line from London to Plymouth was begun. It followed the same route as the Portsmouth line but branched off at Chatley Heath. The first station was at Worplesdon where a tower was built in St Mary's Churchyard and there was another on the Hog's Back, the site of today's Hog's Back Hotel. The line was never completed and fizzled out at Romsey.

It is debatable how much the system was actually used. Top secret messages were sent in document form on mailcoaches. There were plans for it to be used by the public to send commercial messages, but this was never adopted.

The last semaphore messages, visibly clacking away through the countryside – the 19th century equivalent of today's internet super-highway – were sent in 1847 after which it was replaced by a far quicker and more reliable system – the electric telegraph.

Nothing remains of the Worplesdon semaphore tower which was pulled down soon after the system was abandoned. Pewley Hill, now Grade II-listed, became a residential property and was extended outwards with two wings and a dome was added on top of its tower.

Chatley Heath semaphore tower was restored by Surrey County Council in 1989 and is open to the public on certain Sundays and bank holidays, with occasional demonstrations showing how the system worked. It can be reached by a footpath from the car park on the southbound A3, near junction 10 of the M25, at Wisley.

BOOKER'S TOWER

STANDING in the far corner of The Mount Cemetery overlooking the graves of many of Guildford's Victorian townsfolk is Booker's Tower. This eight-sided monument built of Bargate stone bears a cast-iron plaque with a date of 1839.

Charles Booker who lived in Quarry Street and who is included among the town's nobility, gentry and clergy, in Pigot's *Directory of Surrey* for 1839, erected it. He was a corn merchant and miller at the Town Mills. Booker was also a town councillor supporting the Whig party and later the Liberals. A commemorative plaque in Holy Trinity Church states that he was three times Mayor of

Booker's Tower in the far corner of The Mount Cemetery.

Booker's Tower.

sons. He leased about 40ft of land, then known as Cradle Fields, near The Mount, from a Dr James Steadman, and had a 70ft tower built.

Early photographs show that the top of the tower was originally crenellated. A lightning conductor rose even higher. At its opening ceremony a canon was fired and

The Booker family tomb in Holy Trinity churchyard.

Guildford, but his is a sad story. He and his wife, Harriet, had two sons, but both died at the age of 15 years.

A hand-written note in the archives of the *Surrey Advertiser* says that one son, Charles Collyer Booker, died of smallpox on 15 December 1824. The other, Henry Booker, was drowned after falling into the River Wey near the town wharf. Their tomb is in Holy Trinity Churchyard.

According to the note, Charles Booker was determined to build something as a memorial to his

there were fireworks. Flags were flown from the tower on public occasions until the cemetery was consecrated in 1856. During World War Two it was used as a lookout for enemy aircraft.

Local people called the tower Booker's Folly, but he replied, 'a man can do what he likes with his own'.

It is said that he would invite a few friends to join him at the top of the tower where they would watch the

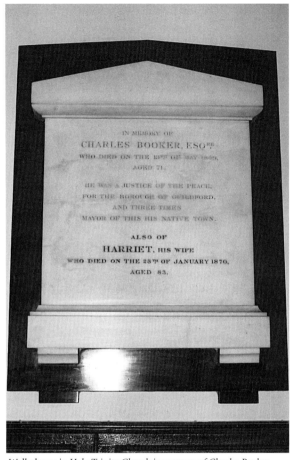

Wall plaque in Holy Trinity Church in memory of Charles Booker.

'Woking railway'. Presumably they stood there looking north hoping to catch a glimpse or a puff of smoke several miles away from the then new-fangled steam locomotives that ran on the London to Southampton line via Woking Common station.

Charles Booker did not live to see the railway arrive at Guildford. Neither did he have long to enjoy the fine views from his tower, as he passed away on 18 May 1840, aged 71.

He claimed that he built his tower to perpetuate his name as both his children had gone before him. He would surely be pleased to know that although 160 years have passed, Charles Booker has not been forgotten.

BONFIRES AND RIOTS

REMEMBER, remember the fifth of November. In the mid-19th century law-abiding Guildfordians certainly did, for it was the one-day in the year they absolutely dreaded.

On Bonfire Night out would come the Guildford Guys to wreak havoc in the town – lighting fires, damaging property, letting off fireworks and even attacking innocent bystanders.

Following Guy Fawkes' failed attempt to blow up the Houses of Parliament in 1605, the event has been marked across Britain with bonfire parties and fireworks. In the early 1800s the tradition was somewhat

A 'disgraceful' scene. An illustration of the High Street when the Guy Riots were at their peak in the 1850s.

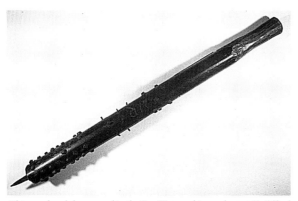

This wooden club was used in the Guy Riots and is now kept at Guildford Museum. Police superintendent John Henry Law helped break up the riots. In 1890 he told the Surrey Times: *'It (the weapon) was a terrible looking thing, consisting of a long stout staff with an iron spike at the end, hob-nails driven into the sides of the wood and tenter hooks around, so that if anyone attempted to catch hold of it to drag it away, he would have his hands torn to pieces. In a struggle a weapon like that would do murderous work.'*

in decline, so many towns formed special societies to keep it alive.

Certain parties in Guildford were keen to celebrate as well, but as the years rolled on they became increasingly boisterous and mischievous. By the 1850s the events can only be described as blatant hooliganism, on a scale that today would see police officers in full riot gear and full coverage by the media.

During the 1852 bonfire night troubles several hundred people congregated in the town, many armed with bludgeons, their faces blackened. For several hours they rampaged through the streets. Afterwards, two Guildford clergymen wrote to the town council to complain demanding compensation for damages to their properties which, they said, were caused by the mob.

When the council refused they took the case to the Home Office, which in turn demanded an explanation from the Mayor of Guildford, William Taylor.

To put it bluntly, Guildford was told to put its house in order and stop the riots forthwith. And although the town council was as keen as anyone to rid the streets of the Guys, tackling the problem was going to be a difficult one as there were few policemen.

There was a plan to enlist special constables to boost

This picture postcard view is believed to be the bonfire on Pewley Hill which was lit as the finale to Guildford's celebrations of the coronation of George V, 22 June 1911.

Up to 10,000 people braved the wet weather to enjoy the Jubilee Bonfire Fiesta in Shalford Park in November 1977. The event officially marked the end of the town's Queen's silver jubilee celebrations. There was a torchlight procession through the town led by the Mayor, Muriel Walls. Providing the musical entertainment were the Guildford Drum & Trumpet Corps, the First Stoughton Scout & Guide Band, the Guildford Sea Cadet Band, and the Cranleigh Junior Brass Band.

Although many people feared for their own safety and their property, it was as if, on the whole, the town encouraged Bonfire Night and all its traditions.

The crowd cheered the 45 Guys who made their appearance in 1860. They wore a multitude of disguises and some were armed. One wore a helmet-shaped white hat with horns; another wore a sugar-loaf hat made of tin foil. A simple black mask covered the face of another, while one Guy's mask consisted of tufts of wool. One even dressed as a woman!

the town's regular force, which in 1851, numbered just three constables and a superintendent. There may have been plenty of volunteers that year, but many failed to turn up for duty when the trouble was about to begin.

The 1850s were a bad decade for rioting in Guildford around Guy Fawkes night. A huge bonfire would be lit outside Holy Trinity Church with smaller ones in places such as at Star Corner and even on the Town Bridge.

The official reading of the Riot Act was the only way to finally disperse the mob. Dating from 1715, it stated that a riotous group of 12 or more who failed to disperse within an hour of being ordered to would be regarded as felons. Anyone failing to comply could be arrested and expect harsh punishment.

During the 1857 riots the Guys lit a bonfire outside St Nicolas Church. The police charged and were met by a hail of stones. In the melée one officer lost an eye. Two bystanders were hit by missiles and another was flattened by a group of policemen, although he was only trying to get his children out of the danger zone!

The years rolled on yet the situation did not improve.

The *Surrey Times* estimated that there were 1,000 spectators who watched the bonfires while suffering the indignities of Guys rushing up to them and demanding money. The event continued until 2am when a lighted tar barrel was kicked around the High Street.

By 1862 the mayor, Henry Piper, was making moves to put a stop to the yearly disturbances. He begged the Home Office to introduce an Act of Parliament that would give magistrates the power to hand out stiffer sentences to people caught letting off fireworks, lighting bonfires, or even wearing disguises in public.

However, it was to take his successor and for Guildford to gain a terrible reputation nationally following two incidents in 1863, that ended the Guys' rein of terror.

During the evening of 10 March 1863, when the town, like the rest of the country was celebrating the marriage of the Prince of Wales to Princess Alexandra, a gang of Guys lit a bonfire outside Holy Trinity Church and smashed the windows of a house in the town. The news of this unprovoked event and that of a drunken

The 1988 Stoke Park Bonfire Night celebrations are in full swing. The event was organised by the Guildford Lions Club and money raised was donated to the Mayor of Guildford's Christmas Appeal. There was the added attraction of a fun fair and the Surrey Advertiser *reported that two people were treated for minor injuries by St John Ambulance and taken to the Royal Surrey County Hospital.*

riot at St Catherine's Fair in October, when about 30 people were injured, spread further afield.

The *Times* newspaper printed a savage attack on Guildford. The mayor was advised to call troops from Aldershot to prevent that year's 5 November celebrations dragging the town down further.

Under the command of Lt Col Grey, 150 men of the 37th Foot, and 50 men of the 1st Royal Dragoons, were dispatched. It seemed to do the trick and the Guys soon dispersed.

Everyone wondered what would happen when the soldiers departed. But this wasn't to be Mayor Piper's problem. While the troops remained, for the next week or so, his term of office came to an end and the new mayor, Philip Whitington Jacob, took up the reigns. He was determined to put an end to the riots.

On 18 November 1863, 151 special constables were sworn in to relieve the troops. Jacob grouped them into zones placing them in parts of the town where they could easily be summoned if trouble broke out.

The Guys arrived two days later. In the violence that ensued they savagely beat up a policeman and Jacob had to intervene by reading the Riot Act.

The mayor persuaded the town council to employ an extra nine constables, plus a new superintendent. He was John Henry Law and one of the first changes he made was to arm his men with cutlasses. Perhaps this and the cold frosty weather were the reason why 5 November 1864, was, in comparison to other years, a fairly quiet night.

The following year was also quiet. Was this the end of the Guildford Guys' reign of terror? Nearly, but not quite. On Boxing Day about 20 Guys entered the town and attacked PC Stent. He ran up the High Street but they gave chase, knocked him to the ground and savagely beat him with sticks and clubs. More officers arrived and further scuffles took place.

Four Guys were arrested and later appeared at Kingston Assizes. Two were found guilty of rioting and causing bodily harm and each was sentenced to three months' hard labour. After that there were no more riots in Guildford.

But who were the Guys? The four who were arrested were all in their 20s. Two gave their professions as painters; one was a cooper and the other a coachsmith's labourer.

In the excellent book, *The Guildford Guy Riots* (Northside Books, 1992), the author, Gavin Morgan, suggests that the activities of the Guildford Guys was largely a rural tradition and as society became more disciplined, support for it faded.

Similar activities took place in other towns across Southern England, notably Lewes in East Sussex. By making the 'celebrations' official the authorities there were able to put a stop to the violence. They are continued in a peaceful, although often boisterous nature, to this day.

Like the rest of the UK, people in Guildford often celebrate bonfire night with private parties in their own gardens. However, a Bonfire Fiesta was held at Stoke Park for a number of years in the 1980s until the Spectrum leisure centre was built. At the time of writing, the Guildford Lions Club was hoping to revive a public firework display in 2001.

There have been other special occasions when bonfires have been lit and fireworks let off. For example, the lighting of a bonfire at Pewley Hill was the finale of the events marking the coronation of George V on 22 June 1911. The official programme stated that at 11pm there would be a 'bouquet of rockets' sending up 'colossal fire pictures of the King and Queen', reproduced in special colours.

At World War One peace celebrations, held on 19

Pictured from left at the 1988 Bonfire Fiesta at Stoke Park: Joanne Gray, one of the Carnival Queen's attendants; Guildford Carnival Queen Gina Fuller; Stanley Cobbett and his wife Elizabeth, that year's Mayor of Guildford; the then president of Guildford Lions Club, Ron Brooking; and Tracy Furlonger, the second of the Carnival Queen's attendants.

July 1919, rockets and flares shot into the night sky, again from Pewley Hill.

In more recent times there were fireworks and also the lighting of a beacon, one of many around the UK, for Queen Elizabeth II's silver jubilee in 1977. In 1995, to mark the 50th anniversary of VE-Day, the borough provided a spectacular firework display which many people watched from The Mount.

And finally, etched in the memory for a long time will be the fireworks that filled the skies over Guildford just after midnight, as we celebrated the new millennium on 1 January 2000.

MARTIN TUPPER'S MYTHS

DID wicked King John really cause the death by drowning of a pretty young girl in the Silent Pool?

The story is centred around England's most infamous medieval king who, while riding his steed, came upon a pool and discovered a local lass bathing naked in the crystal clear waters. He tried to entice her out but naturally afraid of him she swam out of her depth to the middle of the pool and drowned.

For generations, thousands of visitors to this Surrey beauty spot a few miles from Guildford have heard the story. The villain has even been changed to that of Charles II, proving how easily oral story telling can distort the facts. But the facts are that there is no truth in the tale whatsoever.

In recent years historians have been putting the record straight. The legend can easily be traced to the literary work of the Victorian writer and poet Martin Farquar Tupper.

Born in 1810, Tupper was educated at Christ Church, Oxford, was called to the Bar, but became a writer instead and lived with his family at Albury Park.

His biographer, Derek Hudson, wrote: 'The career of Martin Farquar Tupper furnishes the most striking example in literary history of a sensational rise to world-wide fame and adulation balanced by an equally sensational fall to the depths of ridicule.'

For nearly 50 years he was a household name in Britain and in the USA through his book *Proverbial Philosophy*, a collection of reflections and maxims in vaguely rhythmical form. Among his fans was none

LEGEND OF THE SILENT POOL.

Wicked King John, so historians say,
Had heard of the Pool by the Pilgrim's way,
And when to his castle in Gilford Town
On a hunting visit he travelled down,
He soon was told of a nut-brown maid,
Who lived near the way in a forest glade ;
For the strolling Players and Pilgrims good
All spoke of the hovel near Westone Wood,
And of sunny-faced Emma, free from care,
With eyes so dark and figure so rare ;
A rural Venus, the woodman's daughter,
Who often bath'd in the clear, cold water,
Clinging to branches or twining with care
Clusters of lilies in her coal-black hair.
One day, as she swung there, half in, half out,
A horseman appeared with a laughing shout,
And the startled maiden with cries of fear,
Made a dash for the bank and her homely gear ;
But the King was there, and blushing red,
To the deeper water she quickly fled.

"Will you foil me thus ? " said angry John,
" I will have you yet, you beautiful swan ! "
Then deep in the pool on his horse he went,
He was feeling sure of her capture now
When she loosed her hold on the friendly bough
And down in the depths of the pool she sank
While the coward King rode out to the bank,
Her young brother Tetbert, searching the wood,
Came, at this moment, to where the King stood.
" Hast thou seen my sister? Canst tell me, where?
And got for an answer ' Look, churl, she is there !'
With one fleeting glance the boy dived in,
Clothed as he was, in his tunic of skin ;
And bravely he struggled, but all in vain,
His strength fail'd to lift her to air again ;
But clasping each other like lovers fond,
Together they sank in fair Shirebourn's Pond.
E.C.E.
Reprinted from " THE KEEP " by permission.

Postcard of the Silent Pool printed with a poem about King John and Emma, the woodsman's daughter.

other that Queen Victoria. Prime Minister Gladstone admired him, but it is said Karl Marx despised him!

The success of *Proverbial Philosophy*, published in four series between 1838-76, was that it appealed to so

Martin Tupper and his family at their Albury House home in January 1864.

many people who before had hardly understood a word of poetry.

He wrote two novels – *The Crock of Gold* (1844) and *Stephan Langton: or The Days of King John* (1858). It was the latter of the two that spurned the myth of the girl drowning in the Silent Pool.

The website of The Tupper Family Association of America states that his most obvious qualities were his

Picture postcard of the cottage by the entrance to the Silent Pool. The legend of the pool must have been told thousands of times in the tea garden there.

philanthropy, his fanatical Low Church Protestantism, his courage and pugnacity, his obstinacy and his family pride. These, it claims, are all traceable legacies from the Tupper ancestry.

While living in Surrey, Tupper got to know the immediate countryside well and in all probability it inspired his historical novel centred on Archbishop Stephan Langton and his feuds with King John. Tupper places Langton's birth at Friday Street; there are incidents at Guildford Castle and Tangley Place at Wonersh, and, of course, the death of the poor woodman's daughter Emma, in the Silent Pool.

Tupper wrote this book as an historical novel, but perhaps the only true connection between the characters and Surrey is when John is forced to put his seal on the Magna Carta (he never actually signed it) at Runnymede in 1215.

Stephan Langton was a best seller, but by the end of the 19th century Tupper, who had died in 1889, was all but forgotten.

Soon there came an ever-increasing number of visitors to the Surrey countryside. With the advent of the motor-car and the motor-bus many more made their way to places such as Newlands Corner, Shere and the Silent Pool. Picture postcards were eagerly bought and kept as mementoes of an enjoyable day out, or to send to friends and relatives telling them what a great time they'd had.

Most of these Edwardian day-trippers would have been unaware of Martin Tupper, but some would have had vague recollections of a story about a king and a naked girl in the pool there. Soon it was being passed off as fact.

A certain postcard featured a poem called the *Legend of the Silent Pool* alongside a photograph of trees reflected in the still waters there. Its opening line was enough to convince hoards of people that the legend had some truth to it: 'Wicked King John, so historians say, heard of the pool by the pilgrim's way,' If historians were now endorsing the tale, it must be true, mustn't it?

The story was retold again and again, by those walking around the perimeter of the Silent Pool or while

The Silent Pool was one of the most photographed locations in this part of Surrey during the heyday of the picture postcard. This view dates from c.1910.

sitting enjoying refreshments in the tea garden of the cottage nearby.

Just being there on a balmy summer's afternoon and looking down through the crystal clear waters to the chalky bottom and gazing at the graceful branches of the beech trees that dip down and nearly touch the water, it's easy to believe, or want to believe, that a sad story with royal connections really happened – especially if you are a young child as the author was when he was first taken there by his parents during a Sunday afternoon outing.

A second legend is also told. It's said that the poor woodman's daughter haunts the place. It's certainly a spooky place to be at midnight!

By the age of 19, I was playing guitar and singing locally in a band – a cross between the Rolling Stones and the gentler folk rock of groups like Lindisfarne and Fairport Convention. We were beginning to write our own songs and one day fellow band member Peter Hollis suggested we should have a go at writing a rock opera all about King John and the Magna Carta. Throwing in some of Martin Tupper's myths at the same time seemed a good idea, and so *1215 – The Myth of the Silent Pool*, was conceived.

After a few stops and starts it finally began to take shape in early 1983. The band consisted of myself and Peter (vocals), Glyn Edwards (drums), George Glavin (electric bass), Neil Dewey (keyboards) and Kevin Inch (guitar). All we needed was a venue to premiere it and a name for this group of merry rock 'n' roll minstrels.

Things soon started to fall into place. George suggested the name Jesta, which seemed OK and Peter's mother, Carolyn Sloane, who became our press agent, arranged for us to perform *1215* at one of the Yvonne Arnaud Theatre's Late Night Xtra shows as part of that year's Guildford Festival.

As a warm up the band was invited to perform part of the show – about five songs – at a Guildford folk club called Horncastle that met in the old Trades & Labour Club at The Mount.

That night we set up our amplifiers and full sound system. The songs went down a storm with *most* of the audience, apart from a few who were only used to hearing acoustic music at the venue. They sat there with their hands over their ears! For the big night at the Yvonne Arnaud on Friday 15 July 1983, actor Timothy Earle was brought in to provide a narrative link between the songs by our director Christopher Masters.

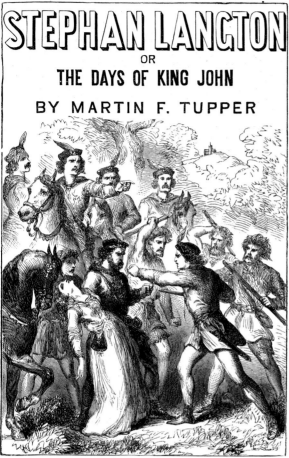

PUBLISHED BY F. LASHAM, 61, HIGH STREET, GUILDFORD.

Swashbuckling stuff. Advertisement from a Guildford guide book of 1904 for Martin Tupper's book Stephan Langton or The Days of King John.

him into a rock music monster, especially during the encore, which had the band's fans rocking in the aisles of Guildford's premier theatre.

Press reviews were mixed. The *Surrey Advertiser* said that musically it was an affair diverse in both style and quality, but an interesting contribution to the Guildford Festival, and with a lot more work would become a good studio show in its own right.

Ray Cassin, writing in the *Woking News & Mail*, said that if your taste was for rock music, the show was fine, although the lyrics did not always match it in quality.

The rock band Jesta who performed 1215 – The Myth of the Silent Pool, *by Peter Hollis and David Rose, at the Yvonne Arnaud Theatre in 1983. Back row, from left: Kevin Inch, Glyn Edwards, David Rose. Front row: Peter Hollis, Neil Dewey, George Glavin, and the show's narrator Tim Earle.*

Our story began with Prince John attending a tournament in Guildford, then the incident at the Silent Pool, followed by John's wicked rule as King of England. It moved on to him sealing the Magna Carta in the year 1215, with the grand finale centred around his death at Newark in Nottinghamshire.

There was plenty of local press publicity before the show to ensure that there was a full house on the night. There had been an appeal for a long-haired young maiden willing to take a dip in the Silent Pool. This was part of a photo shoot from which slides were made and projected on to a large backdrop behind the band during the actual show.

Peter Hollis took the role of King John and turned

It seemed as if the band had put in a lot of effort for just one big show. We did perform it at that year's Bracknell Folk Festival and again the following year at the West End Centre in Aldershot. But we were all young and our musical ambitions lay in different directions. The band split and *1215 – The Myth of the Silent Pool* has never seen the light of day again.

However, Tupper's Stephan Langton does seem to inspire musicians. At about the same time as *1215* was being performed three other musicians/writers – Martin Coslett, Colin Swift and Dr David Lewis, were writing their own work based on the life of Langton, entitled *Song of a New Age*. In 1986 there were plans to perform it at that year's Guildford Festival. It is believed, however, that it has been performed in public since.

LEWIS CARROLL – A WRITER IN RESIDENCE

ALICE'S Adventures in Wonderland is a classic children's story known to millions around the world. Since it was published in 1865, neither it, nor its companion tale, *Alice Through the Looking Glass*, have ever been out of print. They have been translated into almost every language on earth and have been adapted many times for film, TV and the stage.

Most people know they were written by Lewis Carroll, and that he had some connection with Guildford; but few, it seems, know much about this remarkable man, whose real name was the Revd Charles Lutwidge Dodgson, or that he is buried in The Mount Cemetery.

Guildford Museum has long championed his importance and the statue titled *Lewis Carroll's Alice and the White Rabbit*, by Edwin Russell, at Millmead, has certainly added to the town's awareness of him. A further statue of Alice peering through a piece of plate glass is another reminder of him. Unfortunately, it is tucked away in a small corner of the Castle Grounds and missed by many visitors.

The *Surrey Advertiser* often reports matters concerning Lewis Carroll and his connections with Guildford. These have included the centenary of his death in 1998 and other 'Lewis Carroll events' – often staged by the museum. The locally-based film group, Circle Eight, made a film about him in 1998 called *Alice Through The Camera Lens*.

The Revd Charles Lutwidge Dodgson.

Charles Lutwidge Dodgson was born on 27 January 1832, at the parsonage of Daresbury in Cheshire, where his father was the curate of the parish. Charles was the eldest of the family's 11 children. He was educated first at Rugby and then Christ Church in Oxford where he studied mathematics and went on to become a don.

The grave of the Revd Charles Lutwidge Dodgson, better known by his pen name Lewis Carroll, in The Mount Cemetery, Guildford.

He came to Guildford on 12 August 1868, and discovered that The Chestnuts in Castle Hill was available to rent. It was perfect, and the family moved in shortly after.

Charles continued to live at Oxford, but regularly spent holidays at Guildford, especially Christmas and sometimes preached at St Mary's Church in Quarry Street.

The striking Alice statue in a corner of the Castle Grounds.

Here, he took his holy orders and was ordained deacon in 1861, but he did not advance to priesthood.

His father become the rector of Croft-on-Tees in North Yorkshire and was awarded the living of the rectory. However, when he died in June 1868, a new home had to be found for Charles' siblings. Their mother had died in 1851, and as the eldest child, he became the head of the family. Charles had to find a home that would be a base for his younger brothers to begin their careers and where his unmarried sisters could live. It had to be somewhere that was a day's rail travel from Oxford and one that was reasonably close to the south coast resorts and the Isle of Wight – places to which middle-class families like the Dodgsons enjoyed visiting.

Alice's Adventures in Wonderland was written three years before the Dodgsons came to Guildford. Charles was an accomplished photographer and has been acknowledged as the best photographer of children in the 19th century. He never married, but adored children. The character Alice was based on the middle

LEWIS CARROLL – A WRITER IN RESIDENCE

The Chestnuts in Castle Hill, home for many years to the Revd Dodgson's sisters.

In the summer of 1874 Charles's godson, Charles Wilcox, who was aged 22 and suffering from tuberculosis, went to stay at The Chestnuts. Charles nursed the terminally ill young man through the long nights. One morning, after only three hour's sleep, Charles went for a walk on the downs above the town. Some years later he recalled what happened in his essay *Alice on the Stage*.

'I was walking on a hillside, alone, one bright summer's day, when suddenly there came into my head one line of a verse – one solitary line – 'For the Snark was a Boojum, you see.' I know not what it meant, then: I know not what it means now; but I wrote it down: and, some time afterwards, the rest of the stanza

Having a Mad Hatter's tea party. In 1932, on the centenary of the birth of Lewis Carroll, there was a stage performance of Alice's Adventures in Wonderland, *in Guildford. Two little girls, Sylvia Preston and June Morris, played Alice.*

of the three daughters of Henry George Liddle, a Dean of Christ Church, Oxford.

While with them one summer's day, one of them said: 'Tell us a story.' And so he began a tale of a little girl's journey down a rabbit hole to a strange world where she encountered characters such as Dodo, Caterpillar, March Hare, Hatter and the King and Queen of Hearts.

Some of these have passed into everyday speech – 'mad as a hatter', 'grinning like a Cheshire Cat' – terms we use without thinking about their origin. The expressions were probably in use anyway and it is open to debate whether Carroll actually coined them.

His peom *The Hunting of the Snark* is the longest nonsense poem in the English language and was partly written in Guildford.

occurred to me, that being its last line: and so by degrees, at odd moments during the next year or two, the rest of the poem pieced itself together, that being its last stanza. And since then, periodically I have received courteous letters from strangers, begging to know whether *The Hunting of the Snark* is an allegory, or contains some hidden moral, or is a political satire: and for all such questions I have but one answer, 'I don't know!"

The poem was published in 1876 and did not receive favourable reviews by the critics at the time. But scholars and devoted Lewis Carroll fans have been fascinated by it ever since. Many 'psychological detectives' have attempted to find hidden and deeper meanings within all his works. These accounts and theories have sometimes bordered on the bizarre with conclusions drawing parallels with the taking of hallucinogenic and mind-bending drugs.

It has been said that Charles Dodgson was a severe disciplinarian, and although he was a practising Christian, he saw himself as a repeated sinner. Perhaps it was a tortured mind that drove him to an early grave – although others have suggested he wrote himself to his

grave at the age of 66. His sisters did not solely occupy The Chestnuts – there were often other visitors and relations staying there. On some occasions when Charles came to stay at Guildford he had to book a room at the Lion Hotel as his own room at the family's home was already occupied!

Not only did he write books, but he also published pamphlets and word puzzles. Some of these he worked on while at Guildford.

On 23 December 1897, he travelled from Oxford to Guildford to join his family for Christmas. He had a bad chest and a fever. His condition worsened and on 14 January 1898, he passed away.

A funeral service was held at St Mary's Church, followed by burial at The Mount Cemetery. His expressed wishes were that 'there should be no expensive monument. I should prefer a small plain headstone'. His grave is not far from the cemetery's entrance and is well signposted.

The lease of The Chestnuts was retained by his sister Louisa, until 1919 and the graves of other members of the Dodgson family are also at The Mount Cemetery.

TUNNEL COLLAPSE

THE driver and the fireman of a steam train had a narrow escape when their locomotive plunged into St Catherine's Tunnel and failed to emerge at the other end.

A portion of the 120-yard tunnel had collapsed sending down tons of sand and the train of empty carriages ran straight into it. It was fortunate that there were no passengers on board as shortly afterwards more sand fell, burying the locomotive and part of the train.

It was at about 20 minutes to midnight on 29 March 1895, when the train left Petersfield for Guildford with driver Sherwin in charge; the fireman was a man called Stiles, and the guard, a Mr Wilde. It was due to arrive at Guildford at twenty minutes past midnight. Travelling at about 30mph it got about halfway through the tunnel when it hit a bank of sand, bricks and other debris in its path. The first two carriages, being constructed mainly of wood, were smashed to pieces by the force of the impact.

Later, the driver told a reporter from the *Surrey Times*: 'We saw that the signals were all right and went into the tunnel. Steam was, however, shut off, as we were going to pull up at the platform at Guildford.

'We then ran into something and came to a sudden stop. My mate and I were thrown backwards, and I was struck in the back by a large piece of coal from the bunker, weighing, I should think about a hundredweight. We could hear the coaches smash up and my mate got off one side of the engine and I the other and went to the (guards) van, where we found the guard badly cut about.

'My mate went off and told the singalman what had happened, whilst I returned to the engine and put the fire out with wet ballast. The gas (used for lighting) from the coaches was escaping, so I got out of the tunnel as quickly as I could.

'It was a good thing that the gas was not burning in the coaches, or we should have had a fire or an explosion.'

How right he was. If the train had been carrying passengers many would probably have been killed outright when it hit the obstruction. Should the escaping gas have ignited creating a fireball, more would have died, resulting in a major disaster.

About an hour after the initial landslide another occurred which completely buried the locomotive. The driver was lucky as he could have been buried alive when he went back to extinguish the flames in the locomotive's firebox.

All was not well either on top of St Catherine's Hill. Dr Horace Wakefield was in bed at his home The Beacon. A few minutes past midnight he heard a noise. At first he thought his dogs scuffling about in the hall caused it. Then he heard it again. A maid knocked on his door wondering what was happening, so he got up, dressed and went outside to discover that a stable and the coach house had disappeared.

Later he learned that two of his horses had perished as the land subsided and four carriages had fallen into the large hole of the tunnel below. When the second landslip took place, his summerhouse also toppled into the hole.

The following morning an inquisitive reporter from the *Surrey Times* chanced his luck and entered the tunnel from the Peasmarsh end. He later wrote: 'Although it was rumoured that the tunnel was dangerous, in view of the possibility of further subsidence, I ventured on Saturday morning to enter it to see, if possible, what the effects of the subsidence had been on the train.

'For nearly two-thirds of the length of the tunnel everything was all right. But beyond that point the whole tunnel is completely blocked up with yellow sand from which three of the carriages are protruding.

'The first of the carriages, nearest the subsidence, is smashed to pieces; the sides are bulging out and a great portion of the carriage is splintered into matchwood. The next carriage is less seriously smashed, but part of the roof is broken off and lying on the down-line.'

Plans were swiftly put in place to maintain a service

Artist's impression of the collapse of St Catherine's Tunnel showing the engulfed stables and coach house of The Beacon.

to passengers. It was, after all, a market day and a half-day holiday for many people. A lot of people were expected to be travelling on the trains, added to the fact that a large number of football supporters were expected at Guildford to watch the final of the Surrey Senior Cup between Weybridge and Croydon.

A wooden platform was erected on the Saturday morning at the Peasmarsh end where trains from the direction of Portsmouth and Horsham terminated. Trains from Redhill were allowed as far as Shalford station. At both places horse-drawn buses were waiting to take passengers by road to Guildford station. They returned with passengers who had alighted at Guildford but were on their way south or east. A fantastic new invention helped the co-ordination of all these temporary arrangements – the telephone.

About 100 men were brought in whose task it was to shift the 1,000 tons of sand and debris from the tunnel and to shore up the roof.

Mr Stredwick, an engineer with the London & South Western Railway, estimated that it would take two weeks to clear the tunnel. He was bold enough to tell the newspapers that the cause of the collapse was due to a burst water main at the unfortunate Dr Wakefield's house above the tunnel. In fact, the burst had only occurred when the subsidence happened and the conclusion later reached was that timbers used in the tunnel's construction had rotted resulting in an uneven stress being placed on its brick lining.

On the Sunday many sightseers went to St Catherine's hoping to see the scene of the mini-disaster. Within eight days the navvies had dug out the sand and recovered the bodies of the two horses. The locomotive had been pulled out and trains were running on one of the two lines.

Another incident occurred on this part of the railway line in August 1954 when the road bridge over the line between the Chalk Tunnel and St Catherine's Tunnel collapsed on to the track and severely disrupted trains on what was a busy summer Saturday for the railways.

During the golden age of railway construction in the 1840s and '50s the thought of a railway line being laid near someone's land sometimes led to much anger.

Published in the *Times* on 11 March 1850, was a letter about the railway and St Catherine's Hill from a man who signed himself as Semper Virens. It makes interesting reading and one can't help thinking what he would have made of the tunnel's collapse. Part of it is reproduced here:

Sir, About three years ago a lady, a cousin of mine, took a cottage close to Guildford.

This cottage was substantially built, was surrounded by a nice flower garden, and stood on the last spur of the range of hills which overlook Guildford and the Godalming valley; in short, the situation was beautiful and the view lovely, when I say that the cottage stood on the slope of the hill under the ruined church of St Katherine (sic) at Braboeuf.

Well, I went out of England, and in my absence often thought of my cousin and her charming cottage, and wished, as every true grumbling Englishman is sure to wish, that I were back in England, lying on my back in the garden at Guildford, smoking my weed (for this lady allowed that nasty practice out of doors), and admiring the view throughout the livelong summer day.

Sightseers make their way along Portsmouth Road to St Catherine's hoping to witness the scene of the collapsed tunnel. A horse-drawn bus ferried passengers to and from Peasmarsh and Guildford railway station while the tunnel was cleared of sand and debris.

Cottages at St Catherine's near the railway tunnel, c.1900.

A bird's-eye view of the southern entrance to St Catherine's Tunnel today; with a train making its way towards Guildford.

Not very long ago I returned to Old England, and one of the first journeys I took was to Guildford to look after my cousin and her cottage.

As I neared the hill and saw the cottage from a distance, it certainly struck me as woefully out of repair, and I reproached my cousin for stingyness in paint and whitewash, but it was not till I reached the gate that I could make up my mind that the building was what it is, a tumble-down ruin.

The cause of this destruction was soon explained. About the time I left England the South-Western Railway began to bore through that portion of St Katherine's-hill which lies immediately under the cottage. My cousin speedily evacuated the place; indeed, if she had not done so, it would have tumbled about her ears, for it looks now for all the world like a house that has been mined and blown up.

There it stands, torn, and rent, and shattered in

every direction, almost every train that passes bringing down a bit.

Of course it was no use looking for my cousin in the ruin; so, having ascertained her whereabouts from some of the neighbours, and having smoked a weed in the desolate garden, and consoled myself with the lovely view, which still remains in spite of the railway, I returned to town, hugging myself at not being the tenant of a cottage on a hill under which a railway is extended, the more so as I was credibly informed that the company have paid no compensation to the owner of this cottage, who will, I suppose, have to trust for justice to the tender mercies of a jury.

BEATING OF THE BOUNDS

THE beating of the bounds is a centuries-old custom in which folk, in procession, walked the boundary of their parish armed with willow rods to rap trees, walls, fences and boundary stones. The ritual, which has its origins in a religious custom no less, once involved the bumping of children against these objects!

The perambulation of the bounds, to give it an older name, traditionally took place at Rogationtide, just before Ascension Day – which falls 40 days after Easter.

Somewhere along the route a service would be held; the crops would be blessed and prayers offered for a fruitful harvest.

Not only would landmarks receive a whack from the multitude of sticks carried by the walkers, but some, such as a large oak tree, would have been marked with a sign of the cross.

The occasion of the beating of the bounds was also used to check that a boundary was still in place. With no maps available field boundaries, paths and trackways

Crossing the River Wey at St Catherine's during the 1905 beating of the bounds.

Boundary stone at the junction of White Lane and One Tree Hill.

a portion of St Nicolas. In 1832 the borough was enlarged. There was further expansion in 1887, and again in 1904 (when areas of Stoke were included), 1922 (Guildford Park and Onslow Village), 1933 (Merrow) and again in 1954. The last alteration came in 1974 when town and county councils throughout the UK were reorganised. Here, the town's old Borough Council and the Guildford Rural District Council united to become the new Guildford Borough Council.

With willow staves in hand, walkers set off from Compton Corner on the Hog's Back to beat the bounds in 1933.

were often the only indication of where one parish ended and another began. These boundaries had to be stored in the memories of the parishioners themselves, so the annual trip was a useful time to initiate the younger members of the community.

It is believed that in some instances axes were carried to demolish any building illegally erected on common land belonging to the parish.

No records survive suggesting that the bounds were beaten in and around Guildford in ancient times, but the custom was carried out in the late 19th century – probably more for fun than anything else. Today there is a network of public footpaths around the borough, so anyone can beat the bounds whenever they like.

At the time of *Domesday Book* in 1086 most of Guildford's 750 inhabitants probably lived where today's High Street is. By the 18th century the town was made up of three parishes – Holy Trinity, St Mary and

Perhaps someone in 1887 (the year of Queen Victoria's golden jubilee) learned of the ancient custom of the beating the bounds and persuaded the then mayor, Mr Swaine, and his fellow worthies, to give it a try. And so they did, followed by many local schoolboys clutching their willow sticks.

In 1933 the Mayor, William Harvey, decided to beat the new enlarged boundary. Twenty-seven adults and 20 children set off from Compton Corner on the Hog's Back on the morning of 7 June. The course, often through dense hedgerows and thickets and through some quite marshy ground, was about 18 miles in length and enclosed an area of 7,172 acres. It took them 11½-hours to complete the circuit.

Recalling the event 50 years afterwards, a Mr A.J. Hunt, who was a local newspaper reporter in the 1930s, said that the oldest walker was Walter Long, then aged almost 70 and the youngest Alfred Short, who was aged 12.

They all met up at the Guildhall at 8am where they were given willow staves and were taken by bus to the starting point. Here a swarm of bees threatened to join them on route!

The 1933 boundary beaters enjoy a 20-minute journey along the River Wey in a horse-drawn barge to Broad Oak Bridge, near the Woking parish boundary.

His chaplain, the Revd J. Lloyd Davies, and Maurice Quittenton, bumps the Mayor of Guildford, William Harvey, three times on the boundary stone at Compton.

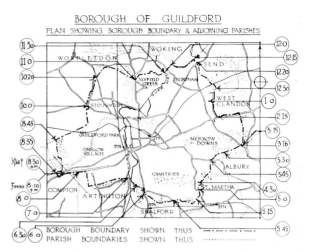

BOROUGH OF GUILDFORD
PLAN SHOWING BOROUGH BOUNDARY & ADJOINING PARISHES

P.T.O. for Programme.

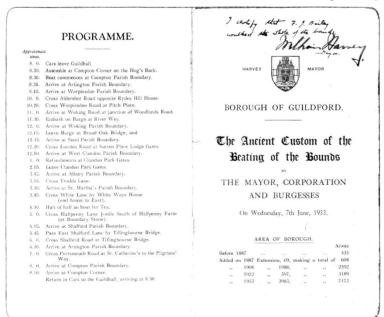

The programme for The Ancient Custom of the Beating of the Bounds, *Wednesday 7 June 1933, owned by Dorothy Wright whose father, Fred Bailey, took part. The mayor confirmed that Mr Bailey walked the whole of the bounds by signing it. Fred Bailey owned a tobacco and confectionery business in Guildford for many years.*

Mr Hunt said: 'The beat began at the Compton parish boundary where the mayor was bumped three times against the boundary stone by his chaplain, the Revd J. Lloyd Davies and Maurice Quittenton. At the second boundary stone (they were now heading in a northerly direction) the mayor got even with his chaplain by bumping him with the help of a councillor.

'A schoolboy was the next victim at the Worplesdon parish boundary. On reaching the Aldershot Road, near Rydes Hill House, the mayor's daughter, Betty Harvey, was bumped by the oldest and the youngest of the beaters.'

He pointed out that: 'Chitty's Common, Worplesdon, provided the first serious impediment to the walkers as they struggled to cross marshy hollows, several of them sinking in malodorous sludge until it covered their ankles.'

A lunch stop was enjoyed in the Slyfield Green area with the party then moving on towards the River Wey. Near Stoke Lock there was what Mr Hunt described as, a giant barge drawn by a solitary horse. It

Boundary stone at the foot of St Catherine's Hill by the River Wey.

Boundary Stone near St Martha's Hill.

Having a rest on a very hot day – 7 June 1933.

The author (far left) and friends who took part in their own unofficial beating of the Stoughton bounds in 1984, pictured in the garden of the Cricketers pub at Rydes Hill.

was waiting to take the walkers on a leisurely 20-minute cruise down stream. They moored at Broad Oak Bridge where they were met by members of Ripley and Send parish councils and then made their way once more on foot past Sutton Place and across what is now the A3 towards the parish boundary with West Clandon.

The route then went through the grounds of Clandon Park where the hungry walkers enjoyed delicious sandwiches provided by Lord and Lady Onslow. It was then on past Merrow and towards St Martha's parish through some pretty dense undergrowth.

Tea was enjoyed in a field near Halfpenny Lane and they then made their way towards the parish of Artington, mainly following the Tillingbourne stream. The River Wey was crossed at St Catherine's and the walkers then made their way across the Portsmouth

Road and followed the Pilgrims' Way back to Compton. No doubt they were tired but satisfied, and here a bus was waiting to take them all back to the Guildhall.

In the 1970s the Surrey group of the Long Distance Walkers Association mapped out a new Guildford Boundary Walk, using existing public footpaths and trackways. The group organised annual walks of the circuit that were advertised as an interesting and scenic 22-mile challenge walk. And so it is. Everyone, who can do so, should try this walk at least once in his or her lifetime.

However, the Guildford borough boundary is not the only boundary in the vicinity that has seen boundary beaters upon it. On a number of Boxing Days in succession during the 1980s the author, with a group of friends, undertook their own annual, but quite unofficial, beating of the Stoughton boundary. Completed purely for pleasure as a seasonal walk rather than to remind ourselves where the real boundary lay, we certainly did not carry axes to demolish any 'illegal' buildings in our path!

Our perambulation began at the Wooden Bridge pub and followed a route roughly around the ward of Stoughton (and a bit of Bellfields), bordering Whitmoor Common, Rydes Hill and down the Aldershot Road, beside Westborough ward, and back to our starting point. The first stretch was tricky as it was a bit dry, i.e. no pubs! The second half was more welcoming as it included the Ship at Pitch Place, the Cricketers at Rydes Hill, and enough time for a quick drink in the Holroyd Arms along the Aldershot Road before heading back to the 'Bridge' for a final jar, or two.

A WORLD FAMOUS DAIRY
– COW & GATE

A SIMPLE illustration featuring a cow looking over a gate helped a Guildford dairy firm become famous throughout the world.

Brothers, Charles Arthur and Leonard Gates inherited their father's grocery and dairy business in the 1880s. Called The West Surrey Central Dairy Company,

Terracotta cream pot with original paper label of The West Surrey Central Dairy Company.

its trademark had been a pair of wrought-iron gates. In about 1891 the brothers decided to update this design and cut out illustrations from newspapers and magazines hoping for some inspiration. There just happened to be a picture of a farmyard gate and another of a cow. And, as if by magic, once they had been placed one on top of the other, a new emblem was born. Having the surname Gates may have helped consolidate what today's advertising people call the 'branding' of their product. However, the business remained The West Surrey Central Dairy Company for nearly 40 years, Cow & Gate Ltd was not registered as a trade mark until 1929.

The humble origins of the Gates' family business go back to 1771, with a grocery shop in the High Street. They were also wine and spirit merchants and, in 1881, offered beverages from no less than 40 brewers.

Soon after Charles Gates handed over the business to his two sons they dispensed with alcoholic drinks. They had found religion and as a sign of their commitment to their beliefs tipped the last of their stock into the gutter outside the shop for all to see.

With their cellars now empty of the 'demon drink' and technology in the form of a newly-invented milk separating machine to help make cream, the Gates brothers opened their first dairy. They bought milk from local farms and made it into 'pure rich thick cream'. This was sold in little brown jugs with a paper label that featured a picture of the soon-to-be-famous cow looking over a gate.

View looking down the High Street with Gates' grocery store on the right c.1900.

In the 1900s a new product – dried milk – reached Britain from the USA. By 1905, Gates were proudly selling their Dried Pure English Milk, from the family

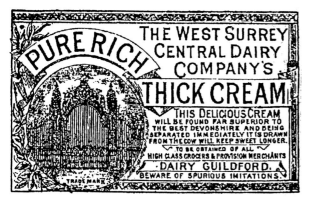

Advertisement for the West Surrey Central Dairy Company incorporating the original trade mark of a pair of wrought-iron gates.

shop in the High Street (where Wax Lyrical the candle shop is today). The shop was modernised prior to 1912 and in that year it boasted high-class groceries, provisions and dairy dainties 'which can now be obtained at the lowest London store prices, together with the best possible service'. Four years later a fire broke out in a storeroom at the rear of the shop. Although the fire brigade was at the scene within minutes, they were unable to save it.

Next door, the Three Pigeons pub was also gutted

The original registered trademark of Cow & Gate Ltd.

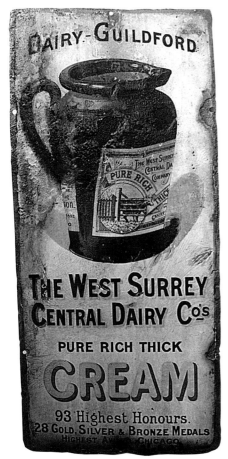

Enamel advertising sign for The West Surrey Central Dairy Company featuring one of its distinctive brown cream jugs.

The Smiler trade mark.

Advertisement for Gates published in Homeland Handbooks' Guide to Guildford *(1914 edition). The artist made the High Street shop front appear much larger than it really was.*

Stoneware jar of C.A. & L. Gates dating from the 1890s.

and later rebuilt. However, firemen prevented the blaze causing too much damage to Abbot's Hospital.

Charles Arthur Gates died in April 1919. In reporting his death the *Surrey Times* said that he 'was associated with the Plymouth Brethren religious group in Guildford for many years'. The report added that his simple funeral service at Stoughton Cemetery was 'without ceremony'.

In the 1920s Gates moved to larger premises in Central Buildings around the corner in North Street. By now the business was growing rapidly and there were creameries in Somerset, Dorset and Ireland. In later years Cow & Gate had offices in Epsom Road. In 1959 it merged with United Dairies to form Unigate.

Generations of babies and young children worldwide have been weaned on Cow & Gate products. The 'Smiler' trade mark of a baby wearing a crown, along with the slogan 'the food of royal babies', was introduced in 1930.

Today every supermarket stocks Cow & Gate baby food products, although the company is now based at Trowbridge in Wiltshire and in Eire.

A DROP OF THE HARD
AND THE SOFT STUFF

TOWARDS the end of the 19th century you could drink beer from at least half a dozen different Guildford breweries. And if your thirst was for non-alcoholic drinks, then during the early years of the 20th century, there were at least nine different mineral water firms here.

Now there are no breweries or soft drinks manufacturers in the town and much of what we consume is made hundreds of miles away by huge multi-national companies. How different it was 100 years ago when you knew that the pint of beer you were drinking was brewed on your doorstep and that pure

A view from the Town Bridge in the 1860s showing Crooke's Brewery (left) on the west bank of the River Wey.

The Friary Brewery in its formative years with the building that had started out as a steam flour mill.

fresh spring water from the Surrey Hills was used to make your fizzy lemonade that came in bottles with a glass marble stopper, bought from your local corner shop.

A good supply of water, hops and malt were available for beer making and it was drunk in large quantities. About 80 pubs and beer shops were established in the town during the 19th century. Some are still with us today, such as the Kings Head in Stoke Road, or the Rats Castle in Sydenham Road, others have long gone including the Crown in North Street and the Dolphin in Chertsey Street.

Within the last couple of years some of Guildford's pubs have changed considerably. The age of the pub company is upon us. They have altered 'traditional' pubs turning them into theme-type bars. What was once the Two Brewers has now become the Mash Tun (it was

briefly the Old Guildfordian) and the Mary Rose is now the Five & Lime.

Friary Meux was once the town's main brewery. It was situated between Onslow Street and Commercial Road and brewed its last pint in Guildford in 1969. Its history in the town goes back as far as the early 1870s when Charles Hoskin Master went into partnership with Thomas Taunton, another brewer who was already established here.

The pair did not make good business partners and within a year Master was running the brewery on his own. Over the next 20 years other smaller breweries in neighbouring towns were bought out until it was trading as Friary, Holroyd & Healy's Brewery. The company merged with Meux in 1956 to become Friary Meux.

In the closing years of the 19th century Guildford's

Choose your takeaway. Victorian stone jars from a number of different Guildford breweries and wine and spirit merchants. They include Charles Cheel, F.A. Crooke, Jesse Boxall, Nealds & Cooper, Lascelles Tickner, J.F. Kitchen, Friary, and J. Kettle.

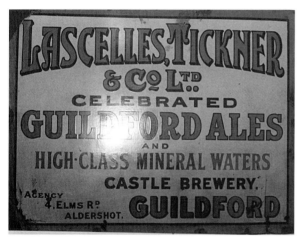

Lascelles Tickner & Co Ltd, enamel advertising sign for its 'celebrated Guildford ales and high-class mineral waters'. Signs like these now go by the delightful name of street jewellery.

early 19th century and continued until it was bought out by Hodgsons' Kingston Brewery in 1929. It was situated on the west bank of the River Wey near the Town Bridge approximately where a car park is today, beside the George Abbot pub.

The Stoke Brewery was on a site between North Street and Chertsey Street and it is believed to have been founded in the late 1830s by Thomas Chennel, whose family were corn factors, millers and maltsters. By the 1850s it was run by Thomas Bowyer, whose relatives were also involved in milling. They owned Stoke Mill for many years.

A half-pint Friary beer bottle dating from c.1900 pictured alongside an ashtray advertising Friary Ale.

second largest brewery was Lascelles Tickner & Co's Castle Brewery. It was situated at the foot of Portsmouth Road near St Nicolas Church and was formed from two other breweries that had been in the hands of the Taunton family – the Castle and the Cannon breweries.

Like the Friary Brewery, Lascelles Tickner & Co owned a number of tied houses in Guildford and further afield, but the latter also produced mineral waters. Friary eventually bought out its biggest rival in 1927.

Another brewery that owned a string of pubs was Crooke's. It was a family-run business that started in the

The 1890s saw a rush of activity as larger town breweries began to swallow up smaller ones. The *Surrey Advertiser* of 15 March 1890, carried an advertisement stating that F.A. Crooke & Co had taken over the Stoke Brewery. Strangely, in the same issue but on another page was the regular advert for the Stoke Brewery, which proclaimed: 'Mr Bowyer begs to take this opportunity of thanking numerous customers and informing them he now has a stock of Pale Ales brewed in March, from malt and hops alone, which are in a splendid condition.' The same advert also mentioned his 'beer for haymaking and harvesting for 8d per gallon' and 'XXX Strong Ale at 36s a barrel' (a barrel being 36 gallons).

The Star pub in Quarry Street looks much the same on the outside as it did in Victorian times when Jessie Boxall III owned it. He established his Star Brewery in Shalford Road and owned several other pubs including the Prince of Wales in Woodbridge Road and the Jolly Farmer in Bramley. The business was wound up in about 1894.

Guildfordians were also being tempted with beers

In its heyday the Friary Brewery supplied beer and ales to its pubs situated around the Guildford area and beyond. This advertisement appeared in a 1934 edition of the Guildford City Outlook magazine.

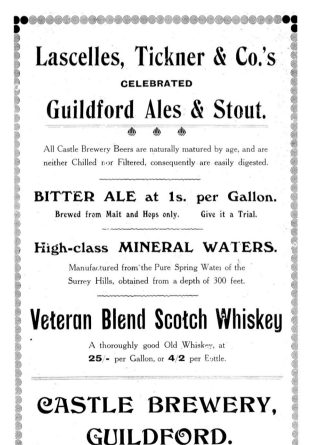

Lascelles Tickner & Co Ltd, newspaper advertisement c.1910.

from other breweries in Surrey as well as from London and beyond. Ind Coope of Romford placed the following advertisement in the *Surrey Advertiser* on 4 January 1890: 'Messers Ind Coope & Co Ltd., beg to inform residents of Guildford and its environs that in order to meet the increased demand for their celebrated Romford Ales, Stouts and Porters, they have opened an office in Guildford.' The notice went on to inform readers that 18 gallons of XXXK Strong Ale could be purchased for 33s, nine gallons for 17s 6d, and four and a half gallons for 9s. Family Ale was 16s for 18 gallons. The brewery offered all its beverages in barrels if required, with discounts for cash on delivery sales.

Another advertisement was rather polite. It was for Webb & Son's Broadford Brewery at Shalford. The

The Crown in North Street would have been well known to the town's Victorian drinkers. It was a Friary pub until the brewery sold it to the borough council in the early 20th century when it was knocked down to widen the road.

company, it said, 'Begs to inform the Nobility, Clergy and the Gentry that they are now able to supply their celebrated Porter and Stout bottled in pints.' The notice added that the brewery had water from Guildford Water Works laid on as its own wells had shown signs of 'giving out owing to the excessive drought'.

By the middle of 1890 Fremlin Bros of Kent, with its distinctive trademark of an elephant, had opened a branch at 70 High Street, Guildford. The Guildford Stores was selling beer brewed by Crowley & Co of Alton, and a grocer, W. Brooking & Son of Dapdune Road and North Street, was selling Amey's Ales & Stouts.

There was so much to choose from it's not surprising that there was, like many other towns, the problem of drunkenness. A look through the local newspapers for the latter years of the 19th century and the early part of

the 20th reveals a lot of what was going on. Almost weekly under the Borough Bench heading are stories of people fined for being drunk and disorderly.

It may be argued that today's magistrates' courts deal with similar crimes; however, in Victorian society drinking too much alcohol was definitely a social nuisance.

A glance at the *Surrey Advertiser* of 1890 reveals that under a sub heading 'Disgraceful conduct' a horse dealer was summoned for being drunk and disorderly in Friary Street and also with making use of obscene language. This took place between the hours of 2pm and 3pm. He was fined £1.

Another case concerned a woman found drunk in Commercial Road. The newspaper reported that: 'PC Gamester said the prisoner's husband complained to him about his wife being drunk. A witness saw her

The Dolphin in Chertsey Street not long before it was demolished in 1915.

standing against a wall drunk and shouting and refusing to go home. She said her husband was on the 'boose' all day and went after him and had a drop of drink too.' The report went on to say that she had been in court the previous week and was then found guilty of being drunk and was fined £1. That she had not paid. The bench was extremely lenient to her and the report concluded by saying: 'On the condition that she took the pledge they would give her another chance'.

Some crimes, the result of too much drink, were more serious. While drunk, a porter from the White Lion Hotel broke into the Jolly Farmer pub and stole 'gold and silver coins, jewellery, 50 cigars and a bottle of port. He was sentenced to three months in prison with hard labour.

Violent behaviour from a young soldier of the Queen's Royal West Surrey Regiment in which a brawl developed and police officers were injured, saw the soldier jailed for a month.

Some of Guildford's pubs look to have been quite rough establishments by their appearance in old photographs. One can picture men (and women for that matter) literally falling out their doors at closing time! And from the advertisements in the local press, it would seem that beer was consumed at home in large quantities too.

The Temperance Movement began in Britain in about 1830 and gained momentum two years later when a weaver, Joseph Livesey, and seven other working men from Preston in Lancashire signed a pledge that they would never again drink alcohol. With several other influential people, Quakers and members of the Salvation Army playing an active role, one of its aims was to persuade Parliament to pass legislation restricting the sale of alcohol and promote teetotalism. The National Temperance Federation was formed in 1884 and became closely associated with the Liberal party – the Conservatives traditionally supporting the interests of the breweries. Many Nonconformist ministers were active in the Temperance Movement denouncing the 'evils of drink'.

The Guildford Temperance Society was formed in 1854, followed by a number of Temperance lodges, including various Bands of Hope (an organisation aimed at working-class children) and a branch of the British Women's Temperance Association.

There was a Temperance Hall in Ward Street which provided a meeting place and nearby, on the corner with North Street, the Royal Arms Temperance Hotel, which was opened in 1881. It was, however, not a great success and was sold to the neighbouring Guildford Working Men's Institute 10 years later.

There were other unlicensed hotels in the town including the Imperial, at the junction of Market Street and North Street, and the Weyside Temperance Hotel, on the corner of The Mount and Portsmouth Road. As an alternative to alcohol, these premises served tea, coffee and an ever-expanding range of mineral waters.

The Jolly Farmer pub situated by the River Wey on the Shalford Road was built in 1913. It was refurbished in 2001 and has been renamed The Weyside.

The Napoleon in Park Street in its final years. During its existence it had been associated with the Cannon Brewery, Lascelles Tickner & Co Ltd, the Friary Brewery, and Ind Coope, part of the Allied Breweries conglomerate.

The art of manufacturing artificially carbonated soft drinks is credited to a man named Joseph Priestley in the 18th century, but it was not until the latter half of the 19th century that the great boom in artificial mineral waters and brewed ginger beer really took off.

Towns and cities the length and breadth of Britain had their own manufacturers who bottled their drinks in a variety of glass and stoneware bottles. Not only was their fizzy pop sold as an alternative to alcohol, it was also a healthy alternative to a sometimes unreliable water supply. The trick was, in the case of carbonated drinks, to stop the contents from losing its fizz and so bottle manufacturers came up with imaginative ways of forming a closure or stopper for the bottle. Hiram Codd's bottle, with its characteristic glass marble held in a crimp within the bottle's neck, is one of the best known examples, but many other weird and wonderful ideas were patented and actually went into production, and Guildford's mineral water manufacturers used some of these.

Frederick Wheeler inherited his father's chemist's

The next
FRIARY
is always
as good as
the last

FRIARY

ALES & STOUT

NEVER VARY

Page Twenty-five

Proud of the quality of their ales and stouts. A Friary advertisement from the 1949 Guildford Festival Week programme.

The chemist and mineral water manufacturer Frederick Wheeler used a variety of stoneware and glass bottles.

shop at 129 High Street and ran it from 1872 to 1904. He also produced mineral waters, which were sold in a great variety of glass and stoneware bottles. Of the latter, most are of a poor quality. They are crudely made, which suggests that they were the cheaper offerings from the potteries of the time. Perhaps Wheeler was a spendthrift. He was keen to get his bottles back from his customers so that he could refill them and send them out again as some are marked with the delightful reminder: 'Please return me to my home'.

His Weyside Mineral Water Works were in Bedford Road. A guide book, titled *General and Business Guide to Guildford, 1892*, points to the fact that Wheeler may not have been so mean with his money, but took an interest in the health of his customers.

The guide book states: 'All descriptions of (Wheeler's) mineral waters are manufactured. Only the finest ingredients being used in their production and these highly refreshing beverages enjoy an unequalled reputation for purity, uniform quality, and fine flavour and aroma.

'Patients suffering from that dreaded disease diabetes, on whom sugar acts as a poison, can obtain from this factory such refreshing beverages as lemonade, ginger ale, etc., sweetened with saccharin, a substance which has not the slightest effect on the human economy, and in fact passes through the system unchanged.'

What a way to put it! But we can draw on the fact that Wheeler saw his mineral waters as having medicinal properties as well as being thirst-quenchers. And with his cheap bottles, perhaps he could sell his drinks at slightly lower prices to those less well off.

At Guildford's town council election on 1 November 1888, three Liberal candidates ousted their Tory rivals. One of the victorious councillors was Frederick Wheeler, who secured his seat by one vote over his opponent.

In a kind of election promise, *The West Surrey Times and County Express,* of 12 October 1888, reported: 'Mr Frederick Wheeler has been connected with Guildford

On the left in this picture can be seen the Connaught Temperance Hotel in the floods of 1928. The building had previously been the home of the Crooke family of brewers.

for over 40 years and regards the main drainage question as being within the immediate sphere of practical politics, and if elected he may tend to the satisfactory solution to this momentous question.'

This is another clue to his determination to see that the people of Guildford had a better drainage system and a healthy water supply – from either the tap or the bottle.

From the 1880s onwards it became easier for people to set up their own mineral water making businesses. The equipment to artificially carbonate water was easily available; fruit flavours came in syrup or block form and there were plenty of bottle makers and firms to supply the machinery needed to fill them.

It seems that three specific types of tradespeople more than any others were connected with this industry. They were brewers, chemists and bakers. As already mentioned, brewers Lascelles Tickner & Co, produced soft drinks, so did chemist Frederick Wheeler, and in

Stoughton Road baker James Collins turned his hand to the trade.

At the time of the 1881 census he and his wife Susannah shared their house with their two children and two other young men, Charles Pridgham and William Piper, both aged 23. Their occupation is given as bakers. In the census Collins is listed as a mineral water maker and baker. It is possible that producing fizzy lemonade was a sideline business, possibly a seasonal one. There was much more demand for thirst-quenching drinks if it was a hot summer.

Another person who must have known a thing or two about baking and catering was Harry How who owned a restaurant in the 1900s at 83 High Street, next to the Town Bridge. He also sold chocolates and confectionery and brewed his own ginger beer and made fizzy drinks.

Another side of his business was hiring out rowing boats and he specialised in providing lunch and tea

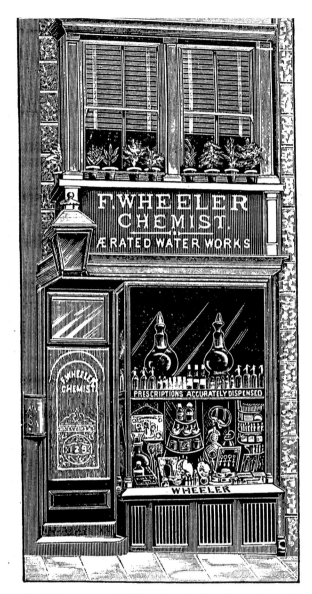

Illustrations from General and Business Guide to Guildford, *showing Frederick Wheeler's shop in the High Street and his mineral water works off Onslow Street.*

picnic hampers which he advertised as 'complete with every requisite, made up for any number'. Almost certainly each hamper would have included several bottles of pop. What expedition would be complete – even if it was just a lazy afternoon spent on the river up at St Catherine's – without lashings of ginger beer!

Some of these old bottles have been retrieved from long abandoned rubbish tips by enthusiastic collectors, the author included; but Harry How's bottles are scarce. Perhaps most of his bottles were tossed into the river after the contents had been consumed.

Harry How sold his 'high class brewed ginger beer' from his shop by the Town Bridge to boaters on the River Wey. The glass Codd's bottle would have been filled with fizzy lemonade.

The Weyside Mineral Water Works was taken over by Edgar Purnell in 1918 and as can be seen from these two early 1920s photographs both horse and motor transport was used to deliver the drinks. Purnells also ran a wholesale confectionery and biscuit business.

Seen from left, stoneware ginger beer bottles of Wheeler, Shelvey and Purnell.

The majority of Guildford's other mineral water makers during the early 1900s appear to have had their premises close to each other in and around Onslow Street. They include Hook & Son and Shelvey & Co. The latter was a Sussex firm that had branches in Brighton, Eastbourne and Worthing.

Shelvey's operation was more than a seasonal part-time venture. In 1906 the *Surrey Advertiser* published a glowing testimonial to the company. Part of it read: 'Home-brewed ginger beer is made from the purest crushed ginger from Jamaica, sweetened with the best honey and sugar. The mixture is boiled in a 100-gallon copper and subsequently passes into vats of 250-gallon capacity, after which purification processes take place.

'Four silver fillers are used for measuring syrup, from which the bottles are taken to the aerated water fillers. The bottles and syphons are washed by revolving brushes, and the casks and jars are placed over a sterilizer connected with a boiler, and steam is driven into the receptacles at high pressure.'

The Ripley-based Stansfield Bros had a factory in Guildford from about 1910-20. Arthur Stansfield had established a grocery business in 1840, and later made mineral waters, but it was his three sons, Arthur, Albert and Abraham, who established the soft drinks business in Newark Lane, Ripley. It is reputed that Stansfield Bros supplied the navvies building the Guildford to London via Cobham line in the mid 1880s with 150 gallons of ginger beer a day! The firm was still in operation in Ripley until about 1990 when it was taken over by Pinks of Chichester. For several years afterwards the premises was used as a distribution point by the new owners.

The ginger beer our Victorian and Edwardian forebears drank was not as fizzy as their lemonade, soda water, potass water or seltzer water. It was also sold in stoneware bottles because of its rather unappetising greenish/grey colour.

After World War One there was a great deal of change in the mineral water trade across the country with larger firms buying out the smaller ones.

Other changes included the types of bottles used. The crown cap had been invented in the USA and was becoming the preferred type of closure for pop bottles, displacing the Codd (marble) bottle and the egg-shaped soda water bottle.

By the end of World War Two Guildford had just one independent mineral water firm – Purnell & Co Ltd, which had been established by Edgar Purnell in 1918. The business was taken over by the Sussex company Fry & Co, in 1952 who continued to use the factory in Stoke Road. And although both firms had been using modern glass bottles Purnell's and Fry & Co, had stayed faithful to the stone ginger beer bottle.

As long ago as 1930 the Public Health Authority had criticised the use of these bottles as being impractical to clean and reuse.

Their death-knell came in 1952 when Winnifred Gardener of Cranleigh brought a court action against Fry & Co in which she claimed she had become ill following a drink from a 'contaminated' stoneware ginger beer bottle. Although the mineral water firm was cleared of any wrongdoing, the subsequent publicity was enough to banish the humble stoneware bottle from Britain. It is just possible that the bottle at the centre of the court case was filled at the the firm's factory in Guildford.

THE CASTLE PLEASURE GROUNDS

EVERYONE was hoping that the weather on 28 June 1888, would be fine for the opening of the new Castle Pleasure Grounds. Alas, it proved to be one of those rainy days in June, but it didn't stop the town enjoying themselves and it was reckoned that more than 20,000 people braved the weather to take a stroll through the Castle Grounds on that opening day.

Lord Grantley had sold the castle ruins, the grounds and the bowling green to the corporation in 1885 for £4,490. A competition was held for suggestions as to the design for the new pleasure grounds. The first prize of £30 was awarded to Littlewood & Aston of London. Runners-up were Cheel & Son of Crawley who received £20, and a Mr W.H. Fletcher pocketed £10 for coming third. The borough surveyor, Henry Peak, worked them into a scheme using some of the features already in place. Local firm G. & R. Smith were contracted to lay the stonework while Filmer & Mason, whose iron foundry was on the site of today's Yvonne Arnaud Theatre, provided the ironwork. When the landscaping was completed, cart loads of plants were ordered from the well-respected Horsell nursery owned by Henry and Carmi Cobbett.

The *Surrey Advertiser* of 2 July 1888, said the grounds 'cover about three acres and that nearly a mile of pathways have been laid out with Farnham gravel'. The project cost the corporation a modest £2,500 and was the envy of other towns, such as Acton, whose own pleasure grounds scheme had, according to the

A print of the interior of the keep by J. Greig, and dated 1 July 1808. W. Clarke, New Bond Street, and J. Carpenter, Old Bond Street published it.

newspaper, cost a great deal more. The report waxed lyrically about the Castle Grounds, saying that the

Early 19th-century print of the keep. The path that cuts through today's Castle Grounds has existed for many years.

mound on which the keep stands 'had been very picturesquely arranged'. It added: 'A waterfall, crossed by rustic bridges, runs down into a lake below, and on one side of the keep itself is a plateau from which a splendid view of the town and country beyond can be obtained.'

There was indeed once a waterfall, but few people today will remember it. The 'lake' was the ornamental fishpond that originally had two fountains.

The subway, leading from the bowling green to the area below the keep, was created at this time. The newspaper report said: 'The sides of the subway are effectively adorned with rockery in which are planted ferns and climbing plants.' It also mentioned two items that have since disappeared. There was once a rustic bridge – near to the Castle Street entrance – that crossed the path which divides the bowling green area and the

rest of the grounds, and a beautiful fountain, made by Doulton's of Lambeth, that was situated near the Chapel Street entrance.

It is believed that it remained in position until part of the grounds was re-designed in about 1910. It is now known that the fountain was sold to Maurice Quittenton Snr who had it dismantled and who then carried it piece by piece to his house in Abbot Road, off Warwick's Bench, in the late 1920s or early '30s. It was still there when, some years later, the family sold the property. The garden was then divided and another house built there, what happened to the fountain after that is a mystery.

The day the Castle Grounds were opened was also the 50th anniversary of the coronation of Queen Victoria and the town was in the mood for a party. The

With brollies at the ready, dignitaries pose for the official photograph marking the opening of the Castle Grounds on 28 June 1888.

Surrey Advertiser reported that there was a heavy downpour of rain after midday, which continued with brief intervals until two o'clock. However, by that time several hundred people had gathered outside the Guildhall in the High Street. At 2.15pm the Band of the 3rd Battalion of the Queen's Royal West Surrey Regiment struck up a tune, but down came the rain scattering the musicians who ran for cover inside the Guildhall!

Meanwhile, also inside, the Mayor, William Swayne, was pacing up and down, no doubt praying for the clouds to roll away and for the sun to shine on the proceedings. By three o'clock it was decided to get on with things and the town's dignitaries in their robes assembled. Led by the regimental band and the town crier, they began their procession down the High Street,

into Quarry Street and then up Castle Street to the Castle Grounds.

Once there, the mayor unlocked the gates and declared the grounds open. After speeches, the band played the National Anthem and a large Union Jack flag was hoisted on the keep and, as the newspaper reported, 'the fountain commenced playing'.

The crowds surged in and the grounds were kept open until 8pm so that everyone could marvel at Guildford's latest attraction. Later, there was a spectacular torchlight procession which assembled in 'the old barracks yard'. It then made its way to Pewley Hill where there was a grand firework display.

As always, at times like these, the whole town involved itself in the celebrations. Streamers and flags were hung from buildings and across streets. The *Surrey*

Looking from the keep to the bandstand, the Castle Grounds fills up with visitors on the day it was opened.

Advertiser said that there were also many fairy lights and Chinese lanterns. The report noted that 'Carling, Gill & Carling (the ironmongers) had a row of lights above its shop window with a gas crown over it, while Wood, White & Tucker (drapers) also had a gas light in the shape of the letters V.R.' However, the *Surrey Advertiser's* report ended in a snooty fashion, by saying: 'A somewhat primitive, but nevertheless, well-meant effort to add to the decorations was made by the occupants of some of the cottages beside the Chapel Street entrance with strips of coloured paper, leaves and evergreens.'

The Victorians knew the value and importance of the castle ruins and its grounds, and some of its history, but it has been during the last decade that much more has been learned.

The motte or mound on which the keep stands was probably built soon after the Norman invasion in 1066.

The keep, made of local Bargate sandstone, was probably constructed in the middle of the 12th century. Partially surrounding it would have been an area of land called a bailey with a garrison including domestic buildings.

There is evidence of a number of royal visitors during the medieval period. Excavations by archaeologists between 1990-94 in the area now known as Castle Cliffe Gardens added further information to our knowledge of the castle and its surrounding buildings. Traces of 13th-century buildings on a site that was an extension to the original expanse of the bailey were found.

Volunteer archaeologists under the supervision of archaeologist Rob Poulton of Surrey County Council unearthed remains of a royal palace. Some of the discoveries were unexpected and Mr Poulton told the

Two views of the Castle Grounds taken at the end of summer 2000.

Surrey Advertiser in February 1993: 'We can now identify the whereabouts of a number of palace buildings including Lord Edward's Chamber, built in 1246.'

He added, however, that much remained to be discovered to understand the overall picture. One clue to that picture came when planning permission was granted for the building of a conservatory at the back of the former St Mary's Vicarage, next to The Chestnuts (Lewis Carroll's former house) in Castle Hill.

In the holes dug for the conservatory's foundations archaeologists found some much older foundations. Made of greensand and chalk, they appeared to measure some four to five feet wide. It is thought that they were the walls of the castle's great hall where important events and banquets took place.

Archaeologists at the July 1993 dig who were uncovering a section of a wall of the royal palace suddenly saw a hole appear before their feet. It proved to be a 13th-century undercroft that may had been used

The ornamental pond was originally much larger than today and had two fountains.

An early 20th-century picture postcard view of the Castle Grounds looking towards the Chapel Street entrance. The large ornamental fountain can be glimpsed among the shrubbery.

There was a bowling green at the Castle Grounds long before the corporation purchased it in 1885. For a while it became a lawn, but by 1907 the bowlers were back. This view dates to about that time.

as a royal wine cellar. And in the November, contractors laying a gas main down Castle Arch uncovered, what the *Surrey Advertiser* reported as, exciting traces of King John's castle.

The trench afforded an excellent opportunity for local archaeologists to look at another area of the castle beyond the excavations at nearby Castle Cliffe Gardens. John Boas of Guildford Museum identified part of a moat and foundations of some large walls in the trench. At the time Mary Alexander of Guildford Museum added: 'I would guess it is all part of the king's suite of rooms.'

By the end of 14th century the castle had been abandoned, the buildings began to crumble and some of the stonework had been removed for use elsewhere. It remained a royal property until 1611 when James I sold it to Francis Carter of Guildford who turned it into a home for himself. It was not the best of buildings to try and convert, and by 1630 he had abandoned the

keep and built himself a new home at Castle Arch. It then had a succession of owners until it was bought by the corporation and proclaimed by the mayor on the day of its opening as 'dedicated to the use of the public for ever'.

With its beautiful spring and summer bedding, the Castle Grounds are an excellent place to take a stroll and to admire everything it has to offer.

How many visitors, when walking through the subway, have stopped to read the terracotta plaque, made at Compton Pottery, that commemorates the bravery of a young man who died while trying to save another boy from drowning?

It is a sad story that had to be researched. The author found it in the *Surrey Advertiser* of Monday 20 June 1904, under the headline: 'Double drowning fatality at Guildford, shocking affair at Millmead.'

The report began: 'A painful sensation was created at Guildford on Saturday afternoon by the melancholy

At one time a large-scale game of draughts could be played in the Castle Grounds. The flared trousers appear to date this view to the 1970s.

intelligence that two lads had been drowned while fishing in the river at Millmead.'

The two who died were Gilbert Smith, aged 13, and Murray Mark Boxall, aged 18. They had gone to the mill pool to fish with Wilfred Henry Apperton, aged 12.

In great detail the reporter told the sad tale. The weather was warm so the boys took off their boots and stockings and stood in the water. Apperton said to Smith: 'Don't go any further'. But unhappily his advice was unheeded. The report said that the lad went a little further and at once fell into a hole. Boxall ran to his assistance and also fell into the hole. Smith somehow managed to climb on to his back, but both sank.

Another boy fishing at the same spot, Arthur Groves, aged 14, went into the water with his rod and called to the lads to hold on to it.

Horace Monk, who worked at Harry How's Old Bridge Boathouse, rowed to the place where the boys had disappeared under the water and soon hauled Smith out. By this time a crowd had gathered and although a doctor at the scene tried to revive him, all efforts failed. Not long after the body of Boxall was found. An inquest was held on the Monday and the

The terracotta plaque that is a reminder of the deaths by drowning in the mill pool of Murray Mark Boxall and Gilbert Smith, on 18 June 1904.

deputy coroner, Gilbert H. White, said it was the saddest inquest held in the town for some years.

It was explained that the hole on the bed of the river had been formed by extra water pressure being extracted from the turbines of the water mill at the Town Mills. Over a period of time it had washed out this large hole.

The deputy coroner said that it was a simple case of drowning and no blame was attached to anyone. The jury therefore returned a verdict of accidental deaths on both persons. As was often the custom at inquests in such circumstances, the jury did not keep their fees but asked for them to be given to the widowed mother of Murray Mark Boxall.

INSIDE THE WORKHOUSE

A GRIM reminder of what life was like in Guildford's workhouse has survived virtually intact, although it was nearly bulldozed recently to make way for new homes.

The casual ward at the former Guildford Union Workhouse still stands behind a high wall in Warren

A green door in an old brick wall. Once the entrance to the casual ward of the Guildford Union Workhouse in Warren Road.

Road. It dates from 1905 and was known as the spike. Tramps and vagrants would make their way to the spike in the late afternoon and queue up outside its large wooden gate. As night fell they would be admitted, given a bath and supper and then locked in cells until the morning.

Before breakfast they had to earn their keep and a number of tasks awaited them. For some this involved cleaning the building – women were more likely to be

Grim reminders of the way things were. The metal grilles through which the inmates on the inside of the casual ward fed stones and flints which they had broken up with a hammer. These stones were then used for road mending.

given this job – the men, meanwhile, would break flints and stones used for mending roads.

Four of the cells were stonebreakers' cells. On the outside wall of these are four metal grilles which, when in use, would have been unlocked and a quantity of large stones tipped into each cell. The tramps were given

A view along the corridor of the casual ward.

designed to be incredibly harsh. Whether a person was in need of poor relief depended on whether he or she was desperate enough to face the awful conditions imposed in the workhouse.

However, by the 1850s it was not the work-shy that made up the majority of workhouse inmates, but the elderly, sick, disabled and children of unmarried mothers.

On entry, inmates would be stripped and bathed. They would be issued with a uniform – made of fairly coarse material. Their own clothes would be washed and disinfected and put into store along with any other possessions they had. These would only be returned to them if, or when, they left the workhouse.

Men, women and children were segregated and occupied separate wards. Often, they were not allowed

a hammer and a pair of wire-mesh goggles and had to break each stone until it was small enough to be fed back through the iron grille.

With their job done and after being fed, the tramps would be released, but they were not permitted to return and stay that night.

It is thought that England's first workhouse was established in Exeter in 1652. During the next couple of hundred years parish workhouses sprang up offering board and lodging and employment for the destitute.

The 1834 Poor Law Amendment Act proposed that all 15,000 parishes in England and Wales should form Poor Law Unions, each with its own workhouse and supervised by a local board of guardians.

The threat of having to 'go to the workhouse' was designed to be a deterrent to paupers. Conditions were

Inside one of the 'cells' in the casual ward. The door has a spy-hole in it.

to talk to one another and could be severely punished if caught doing so.

The workhouse had slang names such as the bastille, grubber, or spike. Some say the word spike originates from the large ornamental iron spike fixed high up on the wall of some workhouses. It may also come from the tool sometimes used for oakum-picking. This chore involved teasing out the fibres from old hemp ropes. The salvaged material was sold to the Royal Navy or other ship-builders. Once mixed with tar it was used to seal the lining of wooden ships.

Guildford had a number of parish poorhouses in the late 18th century that included cottages in Millmead and four houses in Holy Trinity ward.

Graffiti carved into some of the doors dates back to the early years of the 20th century. One example reads: 'And carrots I like man but not the brewer'.

Following the Poor Law Amendment Act, Guildford's board of guardians met for the first time on 12 April 1836. It included the High Sheriff of Surrey and prominent townsfolk such as landowner and MP James Mangles and the banker Samuel Haydon. The area covered by the Guildford Poor Law Union was about 12 square miles.

The law stipulated that no out-relief should be given to the able-bodied poor, but they should be sent to the workhouse. It is understood that Guildford's guardians did not wholeheartedly agree with the curtailing of out-relief and continued to help some of the destitute by way of loans. Many other guardians up and down the country were not so sympathetic!

Guildford's workhouse was opened in 1838 and covered six and a half acres of land. Able-bodied paupers built it. It had its own school, chapel and laundry, and in 1896 a hospital was added for the sick poor of the town. This, along with part of the workhouse, became a military hospital during World War One.

To keep inmates occupied, the workhouse had a crushing mill that produced fertiliser from animal bones.

Life was not easy in Britain's workhouses, but the general perception we have of the regime today may be of its worst examples. In fact, by the end of the 19th century, basic conditions, inmates' rights and the staple diet too, had improved.

The first verse of George R. Sims' poem *In the Workhouse: Christmas Day*, written in 1879, goes:

> It is Christmas Day in the Workhouse,
> And the cold bare walls are bright
> With garlands of green and holly,
> And the place is a pleasant sight:
> For with clear-washed hands and faces
> In a long and hungry line
> The paupers sit at the tables,
> For this is the hour they dine.

But what was Christmas Day in a workhouse really like? Victorian and Edwardian readers of the *Surrey Advertiser & County Times* and the *West Surrey Times & County Press* received a lengthy report each year of the events on that particular day at the Guildford Union Workhouse.

The *West Surrey Times* of 29 December 1888, wrote: 'Christmas comes but once a year and when it comes it brings good cheer, even for the inmates of a workhouse. Hence it is that the advent of the great Christian festival is probably anticipated with as keen feelings of pleasure by those within the walls of the "parish mansion" as by those whose lot is cast in more favourable circumstances.'

The report went on to say that 'it must be admitted that the master and matron of the Guildford & District Union Workhouse (Mr and Mrs Ratheram) did their utmost to secure the enjoyment of those under their charge'.

The day began with the workhouse chaplain conducting divine service in the chapel and the newspaper quickly went on to say that 'dinner, of course, was the great event of the festivities, this being the only day throughout the whole year when the inmates have an opportunity of seeing the savoury joints cut up in their presence'.

Evidently, there was a 'bountiful supply' of beef and plum-pudding. It added: 'After dinner the inmates repaired to their respective wards, where, the ordinary rigid discipline being relaxed to a very great extent for the time being, they were able to enjoy to the full the numerous presents that had been sent for them.'

Among a long list of generous people were: Misses Spottiswood, Shere (framed mottoes for each ward of the house); Mr R. Coe (an abundance of oranges, grapes and evergreens); Mr F. Wheeler (a quantity of aerated waters); Messers Stephenson & Son (snuff); and Messers Swayne & Stone, bakers and confectioners (100 mince pies).

The report concluded by saying that there were 267 inmates, 'so that Mr and Mrs Ratheram had by no means an easy task in ministering to the wants of so large a number'.

There was little change in reporting news of the workhouse on Christmas Day 1906, by the *Surrey Advertiser*. In its issue of 29 December that year, it wrote: 'Thanks to the kindness of numerous sympath-ising friends, the inmates of the Union workhouse – who number about 414 – were enabled to participate in the joys of Christmas.'

One of the Spottiswood sisters was still donating gifts. That particular year it had been calendars and cakes. A Miss Onslow had given peppermints 'for the old men'; oranges had come from Mr W. More-Molyneux and nuts, dates and bon-bons from Messers Tyler Bros.

On Christmas morning the master of the house, Mr W.J. Hill, had visited each ward including the infirmary wishing everyone the compliments of the season. The report said that after breakfast pipes and tobacco were distributed to the men and that the dinner was served in the great hall at one o'clock. It consisted of beef, mutton and pork, with vegetables, and was followed by plum-pudding. There was an ample supply of beer and mineral waters too. For those 'not able to partake in the above more substantial fare', beef-tea was provided.

The reporter finished his article by saying: 'At the conclusion of the feast, hearty cheers were given for the guardians, the master and the helpers. In the evening there was an adjournment to the convalescent room, where singing and dancing were enjoyed until 10 o'clock.'

The plans for the casual ward had been drawn up by the eminent Guildford architect/surveyor Henry Peak as long ago as 1872. It was not built until 1905 and survives today in remarkable condition. Many of the cell doors

A view of the exterior of the casual ward in March 1999, when the building was threatened with demolition. It has since been listed and there are plans for its conservation.

The Guildford Union Workhouse during World War One when it was in use as a military hospital.

exist, although the locks have long since been removed. Many of the doors have graffiti carved in them that dates back to the early part of the 20th century.

The workhouse era officially ended on 1 April 1930, when the 643 Boards of Guardians nationwide, were abolished.

The Guildford Union Workhouse became the responsibility of Surrey County Council and became Warren Road Hospital renamed St Luke's Hospital in 1945. St Luke is the patron saint of physicians and St Luke's mission church stood nearby in Addison Road. Warren Road had, until 1904, been called Union Lane. The name was changed to protect children born in the workhouse from mention of it on their birth certificates.

However, the casual ward remained in use right up until 1962, by which time it was known as a reception centre. In recent years St Luke's Hospital used it as a store.

Parts of the Guildford Union Workhouse were pulled down in the 1960s. When the hospital finally closed in August 1995, the University of Surrey's European Institute of Health and Medical Sciences used some of its buildings. It moved to a new home on the university campus in 1999.

Part of the St Luke's Hospital site was developed by Crest Homes (South) Ltd in 1997, and the new St Luke's Surgery was opened.

Some letters to the *Surrey Advertiser* in 1999 expressed fears that the casual ward building was going to be demolished. The author gained access to it and took a number of photographs for a feature in the newspaper. The article noted that the Guildford Archaeology Group was to undertake a full study of the building making detailed plans. It was then realised that perhaps the building could be saved: subsequently a preservation order was put on it.

Crest Homes revised its plans for the St Luke's Park

Demolition men break up the entrance to the Guildford Union Workhouse on the St Luke's Hospital site in the 1960s.

development. And although safe from the bulldozers, the spike's fate is far from sealed. There are plans for it to be renovated and suggested uses include it being an exhibition centre for Guildford Museum or possibly a centre for the local community.

GUILDFORD'S FORGOTTEN INDUSTRY – BRICKMAKING

I T MAY be hard to visualise today, but at one time parts of the borough resembled a landscape of pits and quarries where adjacent kilns burned with fierce intensity and chimneys belched out smoke. These were the scenes of Guildford's forgotten industry – brickmaking.

Scrape away the topsoil in many parts of Guildford and the subsoil will be ideal for brickmaking; from the thick sticky London Clay found to the north of the town, the deposits of Gault Clay at Artington to the Reading Beds found near Guildford Park. Only the chalk of the downs is not suitable.

In early times there was an abundance of fuel to burn in the kilns. It included the 'lop and top' faggots from felled trees – left over after the heavier timber had been removed for other purposes – and brushwood gathered from nearby commons and heaths.

The Romans introduced brickmaking to Britain some time after AD 43. The fashion died out in Saxon times when timber and stone became the preferred building materials. Brickmaking did not generally reappear until the 15th century when Herstmonceux Castle in Sussex was built wholly of bricks. Towards the end of the 16th century, locally-made bricks and tiles were increasingly being used in the construction of houses in southern England.

There is much research still to be done with regard to the history of brickmaking in the Guildford area. However, a number of local historians have come across scraps of information during their own research projects and appeals by the author in the *Surrey Advertiser* has resulted in some useful information coming to light.

A document held at the Surrey History Centre and dated 23 August 1604, refers to a brick kiln on a piece of land called Martens at Binscombe in Compton. A Thomas Rempnaute of Compton is mentioned as a tileburner.

A further document dated 2 October 1674, details articles agreed between Sir William More and brickmaker Richard Remnant of Compton to allow him to 'digge clay and earth in the Common' for the 'making of bricks and tyles'.

In 1698 at Littleton, Thomas Molyneaux leased land to William Hart, brickburner, for 21 years at £11 per annum; and in 1738 a lease for 11 years at £15 per year was leased by Sir M. Molyneaux to William Farley a brickburner of Binksham (Binscombe perhaps) of Ferny Fields and the Wayes.

Often, brickworks were set up when there was demand locally for building materials. Once the new buildings were completed the brickworks were shut

Aerial view of the Guildford Park Brickworks. The two chimneys can be seen rising above the kiln buildings. To the left are the clay pits with the railway lines at the top. Guildford station is away to the top right and the houses in Walnut Tree Close can also be seen at the top of the picture. In the bottom right-hand corner is Guildford Park Road.

Turn of the 20th-century maps give some clues to the whereabouts of brickyards. On this 1896 edition map there are several marked in Stoughton. Some were only used for a few years while the area around was being developed.

down. The early brickmaker was often an itinerant worker. After the bricks had been fired he might have been employed in the actual building work, or may have moved on to find work elsewhere.

There are other accounts of brickworks in the Onslow manorial records naming Slyfield in the 1830s and at Burpham and New Inn Farm in the 1870s, the site of today's Glendale Drive. It would appear that landowners set up or leased parts of their own estates for brick production.

These small country brickworks operated as to the season of the year. The clay, or brick earth as it was called, was dug in the autumn and left in heaps over winter for frost, wind and rain to break it down into manageable pieces. The winter months were also the time for the gathering of the fuel to fire the burning process. Once the weather had warmed up in the spring the moulding of the bricks could begin. The shaped 'green' bricks were then left to dry in the open air in rows eight feet high known as hacks. To protect them

Not the industrial north, but Guildford Park Brickworks. On the far left the gas works can be seen beyond the railway line. The houses in Rupert Road, off Guildford Park Road, can be seen to the far right. There is plenty of activity going on, but it looks as if the men stopped what they were doing while the picture was taken.

The staff of Thomas Mitchell's Guildford Park Brickworks, in 1929. They are standing on and in front of the firm's steam lorry. A number of names have been written on the back of the original photograph. Those standing are believed to be: Pink, Graham, S. Mitchell, Collings, French, Andrews, Holloway, J. Newman, Capelin, Hope, Hewitt, Sheppard, J. Baker, L. Smith, E. Winter, Woodley, H. Voice, W. Boxall, B. Lee, W. Ford, H. Streeter. In the cab of the lorry are C.F. Emmings and F. Jones. Sitting on the lorry are: Cook, W. Ringer, W. Smith, F. Ford, Roebuck, Unknown, J. Ringer, G. Streeter, W. Hughes, S. Cooper. Others sitting are unknown. Kneeling: Unknown, P. Kingshott, F. Gunner, W. Diamond, L. Liddle.

from rain they were covered with a layer of straw until the summer when they were fired in the kiln, known as a clamp.

To make a clamp the brickburner laid out on the bare ground a floor of unsaleable overburnt bricks from a previous firing. The new bricks were built up on top of this. Up to 100,000 bricks would form the clamp. These would then be encased by more burnt bricks. A number of flues would be left around the clamp, which were packed tight with faggots. Once lit and burning well the flues would be blocked up and the clamp allowed to burn for several weeks.

As it was impossible to maintain an even temperature throughout the clamp, a percentage of bricks were either under or over fired. Even the best brickburner had to accept a certain amount of wastage. Afterwards, the bricks or tiles would be sorted and made ready for transporting to the building site.

The coming of the railways made it much easier to move bricks around the country in huge quantities. A horse and cart used at a country brickyard could only carry about 350 bricks at a time.

As towns and cities grew, more and more bricks were needed. Although bricks would almost certainly

Men at Guildford Park Brickworks in about 1930. Seated on the right is Percy Riddle.

have been imported to our part of Surrey from the large Sussex brickworks in and around Horsham and the huge Kent and London brickfields, Guildford did make large quantities of bricks for its own use. However, there are few visible signs left today to indicate where they were produced. To obtain a better picture of the late Victorian brickfields in the borough we need to compare maps that are contemporary of the period, trade directories and census details.

Taking the Rydes Hill area of Guildford as an example, the 1870 Ordnance Survey map shows several brickfields. Shown here are the census details from 1871 and 1881 for households in the same area where at least one member is engaged in brickmaking.

1871 census

Address: 2 Rydes Hill
Head of house: William Wells, 47, landowner/brick maker, born Camberwell
Ellen, 41, wife, born Guildford
Ellen, Wellman, niece, 12, born Reading
Agnes Farland, 9, born Guildford
Elizabeth White, domestic servant, born Reading

Address: 14 Rydes Hill
Head of house: George Havel, 26, brick maker
Ellen, 24, wife, born Worplesdon

Address: 26 Rydes Hill
Head of house: William Fee, 40, labourer in brick yard
Harriett, 27, wife
Mary E., 6, born Worplesdon
Mary A., 2, born Worplesdon
Alfred Pious, boarder, 23, labourer in brick yard, born Berkshire

Address: 28 Rydes Hill
Head of house: John Crustage, 43, labourer in brickyard, born Worplesdon
Sarah, 49, wife, born Worplesdon
John, 12, son, labourer, born Worplesdon

Address: 29 Rydes Hill,
Head of house: Thomas Holden, 27, brick maker
Mary, 23, wife
Thomas, 18 months, born Worplesdon

Address: 30 Rydes Hill,
Head of house: Henry Dew, 29, brickmaker, born Worplesdon
Elizabeth, 25, wife
Emily, 5, scholar, born Guildford
Harry, 3, born Worplesdon

Address: 32 Rydes Hill
Head of house: Charles Pott, 54, brickmaker, born Guildford
Eliza, 53, wife, born Witley

Not only bricks and tiles were produced at Guildford Park. This terracotta planter is marked T. Mitchell, Guildford.

1881 census

Address: Cottage
Head of house: James Lindtow, 48, brick labourer, born Worplesdon
Ann, 40, wife, born Guildford
?, 21, son, brickmaker, born Guildford
Mary Louise, 3, daughter, born Guildford

Address: Shoemaker's shop
Head of house: James Cobbett, 42, shoemaker, born Godalming
Anges, 44, wife, born Steep, Hants
Frank, 17, son, labour brickyard, born Worplesdon
William, 14, son, labourer, born Banstead
?, 12, son, scholar, born Dorking
Annie, 9, daughter, scholar, born Godalming

Address: Cottage
Head of family: George Goddard, 42, brick labourer, born Surrey
Rachel, 33, wife, laundress, born West Horsley
John, 18, son, brickmaker, born Worplesdon
William Lintow, 13, stepson, scholar, born Surrey

Address: Cottage
Head of house: Montague Bullock, 40, labourer, brick yard
Sarah, 44, wife
Montague, 12, scholar, born Surrey
Emily, 11, scholar, born Surrey
Chester, 9, scholar, born Surrey
Benjamin, 4, born Surrey

The clay pits at Guildford Park were eventually filled with builders' rubble. A car park and houses now occupy the site. Yorkies Bridge can be seen in the background.

Address: Cottage
Head of house: William Revell, 52, brick maker, born Kent
Anna, 48, wife, born Peasmarsh
Richard, 23, son, engine driver, born New Romney
John 19, son, brickmaker, born Kent
David, 14, son, scholar, born Kent
Elizabeth, 10, daughter, scholar, born Bordon

Address: Cottage
Head of house: William Amery, 39, foreman brickmaker, born Shere
Lucy, 38, wife, born Shere
Eliza, 12, scholar, born Shere
Alfred, 8, scholar, born Shere
Haramee ?, 5, scholar, born Shere
Lucy, 3, born Kent
May, 1, born Worplesdon

Address: Cottage
Head of house: Edward Stillwell, 37, brick maker, born Wooton
Emily, 32, wife, born Basingstoke
Emily Jane, 5, born Old Basing
Maria Caroline, 2, born Old Basing
Lily, 1, born Worplesdon

Address: Lidy's Cottage
John Gilner, 24, lodger, brick maker, born Bramley

Address: Stillwell Cottage
William Amery, 19, lodger, tile maker, born Shere
Ben Amery, 17, lodger, pipe maker, born Shere

Address: Rydes Hill/Gravetts Lane, Cottage
Head of house: Charles Mitchell, 27, brickmaker employing 23 men, born Felday

Elizabeth, 26, wife, born Southampton
May, 4, born Felday
Mable, born Felday
Alice Harding, 18, servant, born Felday

These census details give a good insight into those in the community who were making bricks for a living. Difficult to read handwriting on the original census form means there are one or two gaps in the details and unfortunately the house names and numbers do not bear much resemblance to the street numbers of today. However, a walk around the Rydes Hill area comparing the 1930s-era housing to older properties can provide some clues to which homes the brickmakers lived in. Although still classified as small country brickyards, those in Rydes Hill were, by the 1870s, well-established sites.

The name William Wells should be pointed out. He was the owner of the brickworks situated near Chitty's Common and was also a farmer. He was the Mayor of Guildford in 1890 and 1891, and supplied bricks for Stoughton Barracks, built in 1876.

Much of what was his brickfield has now been built upon. The only reminder is the pond behind the houses in Clayton Drive, off Rydes Hill Road, that was possibly dug as a clay pit. Old maps show where other clay pits once were. Again the bricks made on these sites were often used in the building of houses that now stand on them.

Levelling off the land which had been the clay pits of the Guildford Park Brickworks. The University of Surrey now occupies land beyond the trees.

Title deeds sometimes restricted owners of these properties, should they have had the inclination, to start up their own brickmaking business.

According to the deeds of a house on Merrow Common, it still prohibits the 'keeping of chickens and making of bricks', while the deeds, dated 23 December 1896, of a house in Stoughton Road, Guildford, states that the purchaser 'will not dig, disturb or make any excavation of earth for brickmaking'.

The clay found in and around Stoughton and Rydes Hill must have made good brick earth as the *Kelly's Directories of Surrey* list numerous brickworks in the area.

1867 Edition
W. Wells, Rydes Hill
W. Henley, Pitch Place, Worplesdon

1882 edition
Frederick Berry, Stoughton
George Lowe, Rydes Hill
Charles Mitchell, Stoughton

1890 edition
Alfred Bonner, Woodbridge Hill, Stoughton
Dathan Dickinson, Rydes Hill Brickyard, Worplesdon
Robert Earwacker, Stoughton
C. Wrist, 88 High Street, Guildford and at Stoughton

1899 edition
Alfred Bonner, Woodbridge Hill, Stoughton
E & A Miles Ltd, Rydes Hill. Also at Cranleigh – office at Onslow Street, Guildford
William Smith, Woodbridge Hill
C. Wrist, Stoughton

1903 edition
Alfred Bonner, Woodbridge Hill, Stoughton
Herbert Lewis, Stoughton,
E & A Miles, Ltd, Rydes Hill
W. Sharp & Co, Worplesdon (postal address Stoughton)
William Smith, Woodbridge Hill

Page from the midweek Surrey Advertiser, *Wednesday 21 January 1953, and a feature all about the Guildford Park Brickworks.*

1905 edition
Alfred Bonner, Woodbridge Hill, Stoughton
Faggeter, Rydes Hill, Guildford
Herbert Lewis, Stoughton
Rydes Hill Brick Co, manager W.A. Miles
W. Sharp, Worplesdon
William Smith, Woodbridge Hill

1907 edition
Faggeter, Stoughton
Rydes Hill Brick Co
W. Sharp, Worplesdon

1911 edition
Faggeter, Stoughton
Rydes Hill Brick Co
W. Sharp, Worplesdon

1913 edition
Faggeter, Stoughton
Rydes Hill Brick Co

1915 edition
None

These listings clearly show the comings and goings of the brickyards as this part of Guildford was being developed in the late Victorian period.

In appealing for information on brickmaking the author was contacted by Graham Boxall who lives on the Ashington Estate, by the A3 and the Tesco store. When he moved into his house more than 20 years ago and began to dig his garden, he was forever finding old bricks. The more he dug, the more he found. His father had worked at the Hammer Brickworks near Haslemere and instantly recognised this as the remains of a clamp-fired kiln.

Graham dug so many bricks that he was able to build a wall which forms part of a patio and lay several paths through his garden! He also dug up an iron wheel that was once part of a brickmaker's barrow and many pieces of pottery, stoneware and glass.

These shards provide another clue to the whereabouts of long-forgotten brickworks. When moulding the bricks from the raw clay, sand and cinders or ash from coal fires were often added to the mixture. Brickmakers imported household refuse sorting out the bottles and pots, rags, paper and bones, and so on, for the valuable 'dust' that filled up a large part of our forebears' dustbins.

Once the ash had been extracted the left over material was used to fill in the pits from which the clay had been dug. Trying to find a convenient place to get rid of household refuse was a constant headache for authorities as their towns grew – the local brickworks offered a solution.

In 1890 Guildford town councillors were discussing the problem of where to tip rubbish. The meeting heard that there were plenty of farms and waste land in and around Stoughton where it could dump its own rubbish and not put a further burden on the town.

Graham Boxall certainly has the remains of a brickworks and possibly a rubbish tip in his backyard.

Guildford's largest and the final brickworks to remain in operation were at Guildford Park, now the site of a car park and the houses in Guildford Park Avenue.

Thomas Mitchell established a brick, tile and pottery works at Guildford Park in the 19th century. He also owned brickworks at Crondall near Farnham, others in Sussex, and also Seale Potteries. The Sussex & Dorking Brick Company bought the Guildford Park Brickworks in 1929. It finally passed into the hands of Redlands who closed it in 1961, when the works became uneconomic to run. In its latter years it was mostly manufacturing tiles, but did produce thousands of facing bricks for Guildford Cathedral.

Fortunately, there are a number of people who still remember the Guildford Park Brickworks. Here are some of their memories.

George Riddle of Guildford: 'My father worked there and I can remember it in the 1930s. I recall watching the men working very hard, digging out the clay by hand, making and stacking the bricks in the kilns. The men used pickaxes and spades and had to pay for these themselves.

There was once a small brickyard near Newlands Corner, opposite the Silent Pool. Susan Pink of Cranleigh wrote to the author saying that her father, Phil Hedgecock (pictured), and uncle, Jim Hedgecock, worked there in the 1940s. Her grandfather, William Hedgecock, had been a brickmaker at Littleton brickyard. Mrs Pink says that she remembers her father wore rubber mitts on the palms of his hands for protection when he was moulding the bricks. However, he always had horrendous cracks in his fingers during cold weather.

'When the depression arrived, my father was sacked. I remember that times were very hard for the family.'

Mrs D.M. Down of Guildford: 'In 1925 my father, Harry Voice, my mother and myself came to Guildford to live in one of two houses belonging to Mitchell's brickworks. These stood at what is now Guildford Park Avenue.

'My father was a ridge tile maker on piece work and worked from early morning until late at night for over 25 years.

'Many times I went to watch him making tiles. He took "pug" as the clay was called and put it into an oblong wooden box, where it was levelled off, sanded and draped over a block, before being taken to shelves to await firing in the kiln.

'He received a heavy silver medal inscribed with his name and details for long service.

'Each Christmas a party was given for the workers' children. I recall we always had a good tea and there were games afterwards. On leaving to go home, we each received a large bag of sweets and an orange.

'My dad worked until he was nearly 70, when a bad car accident forced him to retire.'

Harry Stacey of Great Bookham: 'As a boy in the late 1920s I lived near Guildford Park Brickworks. There was a path that led to a large field bordering the railway line. There was a tunnel under a trackway in the area of Yorkies Bridge. Clay was dug from this field and there was also a narrow-gauge railway line and on Saturdays and Sundays when the brickworks were deserted young boys used to play on the railway wagons, sending them up and down the track.'

John Essex of Godalming worked at Guildford Park Brickworks as a junior clerk from about 1954-56, before he did his National Service. At that time he confirms that the Sussex & Dorking Brick Company owned it. The Guildford works also administered the Farnham and Crondall brickworks.

Wednesdays were quiet days, the main job was arranging for the loads of bricks and tiles to be collected. When that was completed he sometimes used to leave his office and watch the brickmakers at work. A skilled brickmaker could make up to 800 bricks a day.

There were two heaps of clay ready for the brick and tile makers. A tile maker would take a lump of clay, cut it with a type of cheese cutter and slice it off the mould. Some tiles were made with nibs (the raised edge on a tile), some without.

Another department made ridge tiles. The tiles were not marked with the name of the brickworks but were marked with a number.

At Guildford Park the bricks and tiles were burned in large kilns, a slightly more sophisticated process than the clamp-fired kilns of the old country brickyards.

Mr Essex recalls that in his time there were two kilns – a continuous kiln known as the Manchester, which was coal-fired and always alight.

It had 29 chambers. It took four days to build up each fire. It was on heat for another two days and then took another two to cool down.

Bricks brought in from Warnham brickworks in West Sussex separated each chamber. The coal came from the Bettshanger Colliery in Kent, by the haulier Benjamin Heath. The same firm also delivered some of the bricks and tiles. The second kiln was a Hoffmann, and was not in continuous use.

Under-burnt bricks were used in the wall of the kiln. Some were sold as footing bricks. In those days the works manager was a man named Freddie Palmer.

Mr Essex says that the resident mechanic at the Guildford Park Brickworks was Reg Bullen. He had his 'office' towards the back of the works (nearer to the railway line).

The Guildford Cathedral bricks were made to a special size. They were two and a quarter inches high. Normal bricks were two and five eighths inches high.

The cathedral bricks were normally fired in the Hoffmann kiln. There was a nightshift burner who was a man named Joe Tucker.

By the 1950s the traditional skills of brick and tile making were being lost as more sophisticated equipment was installed. Freddie Palmer was more of an academic foreman than his predecessors. He wanted to incorporate the new technology. The older men would judge the temperature of the kiln by looking into it and working it out by the colour of the flames.

At one time Compton Pottery asked the brickworks to fire some extremely large terracotta urns that it had made. The pottery could not fit them into its own kiln.

A gang of men at the Newlands Corner brickworks. Jim Hedgecock is second left and Phil Hedgecock is far left.

There were various experimental firings, but it was difficult to maintain the correct temperature, so the project was abandoned. Mr Essex says that heat was never consistent in a brickmaking kiln and that the closer a brick is to the source of the heat, the smaller it will end up after firing.

After the brickworks were closed the clay pits were filled in with builders' rubble. Some of the pits had been flooded and a local angling society was called in to net the fish.

The last of the brickwork's two chimneys came down in the early 1960s. The chimney of the Manchester kiln was supposed to have been pulled down by ropes, but came down of its own accord after workmen had removed bricks at its base in preparation for the demolition. Evidently, it was a very windy day. A large click was heard and then a large crack appeared. Very slowly it grew wider; the chimney leaned heavily and then fell to the ground.

A CALL TO ARMS – GUILDFORD'S MOBILISATION CENTRES

AT THE end of the 19th century France and Russia were building warships at an alarming rate. It was feared that our own Royal Navy would be no match for them and that Britain should prepare itself for a possible invasion.

During the 1880s the Conservative MP for Birkenhead, General Sir Edward Hamley, strenuously campaigned for a defence line to be built around London to stop an invader in its tracks should it attack from the south coast.

The Government duly acted on Sir Edward's warning and plans were drawn up for 12 'elementary works' to be built along the North Downs from Guildford to Knockholt in Kent. Guildford had two of the 12 mobilisation centres, one on the Mount at Henley Grove and the other at Pewley Hill.

Sir Edward's military strategies differed from those of his contemporaries. He had noted the rise in the number of volunteer troops – predominately from the professional and middle-classes – and thought that they could be extremely useful in the defence of London in the event of an invasion. His scheme suggested that specially trained volunteer units from the London area could be deployed in the lightly fortified mobilisation centres. However, this idea made him rather unpopular with officers serving in the regular army!

Sir Edward retired from Parliament in 1892 and within a year was dead. Although the land for the mobilisation centres had been surveyed and purchased by 1889, he did not see his defence line completed since building work did not begin until the mid-1890s.

Following his death, interest in utilising the London volunteers waned and by 1905 confidence in the Royal Navy had once again been restored and the mobilisation centres, barely 10 years old, were abandoned and eventually sold off. The question one wonders, is whether they would have worked if under attack?

Should an enemy have broken through Britain's south coast defences and made its way to London, a

Much remains of the original buildings at Henley Fort. Today it is an outdoor education centre run by Surrey County Council.

The steel gates are still in place along with the guardhouse.

condition and visitors can learn about the defence line and the role of the mobilisation centres.

An interesting feature is how these dark rooms were safely lit with so much high explosive around. Candles or oil lamps were placed in recesses in the walls behind plate glass. These were reached by a narrow passage behind the magazine chambers. Upon entering this section workers had to change into special clothing that included soft slippers – a spark from a hobnailed boot could have proved fatal! Once changed they could then pass through into the 'sensitive' area to work.

Long after the military left the Pewley Hill mobilisation centre a bitter row over its usage raged

defence line would have formed roughly along the line of the North Downs. In the plans suggested by Sir Edward Hamley, light artillery guns would have strengthened the volunteer forces (about 2,000 men per mile of line). The mobilisation centres were in effect simply storehouses from where guns and ammunition would be distributed to the troops as the enemy approached. The digging of trenches, redoubts, and so on would then have created a proper defence line.

However, some of the centres, such as Pewley Hill, with a good view of the surrounding countryside, were designed so they could also act as a defence position with an artillery battery. Henley Grove, on the other hand, was more likely to have been an ammunition depot with its storerooms, or casements as they were known, tucked away under the ramparts surrounding its courtyard.

The guardroom, however, was built with a number of loopholes through which men could fire rifles. The centres were never manned full-time but there was a caretaker who lived locally whose job it was to look after any arsenal and tools stored at the site. There is no evidence that artillery weapons were ever stored at any of the centres.

Henley Grove was taken over by Surrey County Council and for many years has been an outdoor education centre, now known as Henley Fort. The mobilisation centre has been well preserved: from its walled entrance (known as a gorge) with its steel gates to its guard hut and the magazine chambers themselves. Some of these have been restored to their original

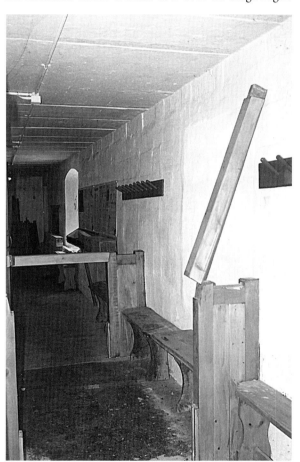

A view down one of the corridors inside the former mobilisation centre. Part of Henley Fort has been preserved to show how the arms and magazine store would have looked when it was in use at the turn of the 20th century. Staff would not have been permitted to pass the barriers until they had removed their outdoor boots and any clothing containing metal objects that could have caused a fatal spark.

Narrow corridors pass between the main storerooms. On the right can be seen a steel shutter. Behind this was a space where a lamp could be safely placed. A window of thick glass separated the lamp from the storeroom. Slippers, like the pair on top of the ammunition boxes, had to be worn when handling explosives to prevent sparks.

between the borough council and a carpet firm. It was the first 'battle' in its history and ended up costing the ratepayer dearly.

It was built in 1895 at a cost of £14,000 and abandoned at the same time as all the others. In 1921 a Mr Lakeman bought it and built a house there with a swimming pool and a large summerhouse. He sold it to the National Building Society in 1938 who converted the house into offices. During World War Two most of the building society's London employees were evacuated to the Guildford area and the underground chambers of the old mobilisation centre were used to store the firm's documents. It was acquired by Hardie Builders Ltd in 1946, and its managing director, Cyril Sharp, returned it to residential accommodation in an Italian style.

In August 1965 it came on the market for £13,500 and was featured in the news pages of the *Surrey Advertiser*. The report said: 'The house is painted pink and boasts an attractive sun terrace with an ornamental wrought-iron baluster. It is approached down a made-up drive into the paved forecourt, with a stone arch over wrought-iron gates, which open on to the stone-paved steps. These steps lead to the first floor which forms the principal accommodation, and has been exceptionally well decorated by the present occupier.'

In was back in the news 13 years later when the *Surrey Advertiser* reported that the borough council had been accused of victimising a carpet firm over the 'battle of Pewley Fort'. The allegations were made by Carpet Decor Ltd over opposition to it using the old mobilisation centre as a place to store its carpets, which it had leased from Reliant Homes.

By May 1980 it appeared that the council had won the row, much to the delight of local residents, when an Environment Department inspector ordered Carpet Decor to stop using the site for storage purposes. However, by August of the following year the case had been heard by a High Court judge who ruled that the Environment Department's decision should be reheard for a redetermination and that the council should pay the carpet firm £2,000 compensation.

Due to the number of large lorries turning and entering the Pewley Hill site, residents feared for the safety of children coming and going from nearby Pewley Down First School.

Finally, the see-saw battle swung back in favour of the borough council. Although it was prepared to go to the Court of Appeal, it came to an agreement with Carpet Decor in February 1983 whereby it bought the carpet firm's leasehold interests for £70,000.

For a brief period the vaults were used by Guildford Museum for storing artefacts. The site has now been redeveloped with housing and the name of one property – The Ramparts – is a reminder of what was once built there.

THE RODBORO BUILDINGS

THE building that may be the world's first purpose-built car factory is in Guildford – and it was nearly pulled down to make way for, of all things, a road widening scheme.

In 1990 the Rodboro Buildings on the corner of Bridge Street and Onslow Street looked doomed. Owned by Guildford Borough Council, it was unused and in a poor state. With an ever-increasing volume of road traffic trying to negotiate the town centre's gyratory system, demolishing the whole lot was one idea put forward.

However, there was strong support to preserve the building, because of its historic interest, and utilise it again. The Victorian Society wrote to the borough council pleading the case for preservation, noting that it was a remarkable surviving example of a purpose-built car factory – possibly the earliest in the world – as earlier car factories, such as Daimler's factory in Coventry, were all converted from existing textile mills.

The building was, of course, saved and is now home to one of JD Wetherspoon's superpubs on the ground and first floor and the Academy of Contemporary Music, above.

It was built in 1900 for the rapidly expanding motor manufacturer Dennis (see following chapter). A Woking firm, Drowley & Co, were the builders, working to a design by an architect called John Lake.

Dennis Bros moved into the building in 1901 and it housed the firm's assembly shop, blacksmiths, paint and polishing rooms. These were on the first and second floors and a special lift took the finished vehicles down to the showrooms at ground level.

In a 1902 edition of *The Gentleman's Journal*, the factory was described as 'one of the most handsomest buildings in Surrey'. As the firm grew so did the building. It was extended in 1903 and again in 1905. But the company was manufacturing cars, buses and light commercial vehicles at such a rate that a new factory was built at Woodbridge Hill.

The Onslow Street/Bridge Street building became a repair shop from 1911, while its main offices remained there until 1919 when the building was taken over by the Rodboro Boot & Shoe Co.

The *Surrey Times* of 17 January 1919, announced: 'Boot and shoe factory for Guildford'. The man behind the venture was William King of Shalford. He told the newspaper that although many people may think it unusual to open a boot factory away from Northampton (one of the traditional footwear manufacturing centres in Britain), he thought Guildford was an ideal place. He said that there were tanneries nearby at Godalming, Bramley and Gomshall, where he would be able to obtain raw materials.

He added that he was expecting to employ about 500 men, women and girls in the factory and production was estimated at about 600,000 pairs of boots and shoes per year – many being exported to Europe, India and China.

The firm, he said, would be making his own patent 'Rodboro' boots and shoes, the difference being that his design replaced the normal inside tongue by a smooth outside one, and that the boots also had fewer lace holes. He got the idea after seeing the problems soldiers had wearing their boots in the trenches during World War

The Dennis factory on the corner of Bridge Street and Onslow Street where vehicle manufacturing began in 1901.

One. He went on to claim that his boots were watertight and a protection against sand, grit and thorns.

The building then acquired the name it retains to this day, but the last boots and shoes made there were in 1928.

By World War Two Rodboro Buildings was a hive of activity with a number of firms trading there. The 1941 edition of *Kelly's Directory of Guildford & Godalming* includes the following: Hogsden Harold, confectioner; Taylors, photo finishers; British Red Cross Society; Guildford Miniature Zoo; Keefe & Lewis, knitwear manufacturers; Charlotte Mann, tobacconist; Prisoners of War Packing Centre; Godfrey Stanley, automobile agents; Clare's Motor Works.

During the early part of the war the British Red Cross occupied a part of the first floor and used it as a packing centre for prisoner of war parcels. Each parcel contained provisions for one prisoner and was to the value of 10s (50p). A parcel included items such as biscuits, processed cheese, chocolate, Ovaltine, dried fruit, jam, margarine, tinned sausages, luncheon meat, steak and kidney pudding, sugar, sweets, tea, peas or beans and soap.

About 140 part-time volunteers packed the parcels on a rotation basis. In total, 171,145 parcels were dispatched from Guildford.

The Rodboro Buildings was also where the fledgling Observer Corps Club was founded. Mr R.O. Dowdeswell, whose stationery and print firm occupied part of the building, formed it. The club was set up to improve people's recognition of both Allied and enemy aircraft.

Early Dennis motor cars with a motor-tricycle on the far left. The firm ceased making cars in 1913 to concentrate on commercial vehicles.

The club's school of instruction was first held at the Rodboro Buildings, later moving to the technical college. In total, 198 other branches were formed and during the war thousands of sets of test cards, folders and journals were distributed to its many members with Mr Dowdeswell becoming Head Observer.

In the 1950s occupants of Rodboro Buildings included: Dowdeswells stationers; L.J. & E.S. Bungey, confectioners; D.L. Lambert, jeweller; Guildford Pet Stores; Keefe & Lewis, knitwear manufacturers; Taylors Ltd, wholesale photo finishers; F. Dancock, tobacconist; Rodboro Hairdressing Salon; Godfrey Stanley & Co, used car sales and motor engineers; and Clare's Motor Works Ltd.

The 1967 edition of *Kelly's* includes Clarke-Power Ltd, sheet metal fabricators; and Bert Webb & Son, who were listed as turf commissioning agents.

The borough council bought the building in 1984

and two years later it was granted a Grade II-listed building status. The outside of the building received remedial repairs for safety reasons and in 1997 work, costing the borough council £1.5 million, finally got under way to renovate the inside and make good the brickwork on the outside.

At that time public opinion was divided as to whether it should have been preserved at all. Most would agree that the work completed here and on the building that has become the Electric Theatre, has been worthwhile.

The Rodboro Buildings is now leased to the public house group, JD Wetherspoon, and the Academy of Contemporary Music. The singer Kirsty MacColl officially opened the academy in December 2000. Sadly this was to be one of her last public engagements as she was killed while on holiday in Mexico before the year had ended.

MAKING SPECIALIST VEHICLES – THE STORY OF DENNIS

MOST readers will have seen or heard a Dennis fire engine and the chances are you have travelled on a Dennis bus. The same applies to people from either Cornwall or Scotland or from New Zealand and Hong Kong. For more than 100 years Dennis vehicles have literally been travelling the world, but their home town and place of manufacturer is Guildford.

Born at Huntshaw near Tiverton, Devon, in 1871, John Cawsey Dennis was working for a Bideford ironmongers when in 1894 he saw an advertisement for a similar position at Filmer & Mason in Guildford. He got the job and moved to Surrey.

In his spare time he assembled a bicycle from parts that he had bought from his employer. He decided to sell it and persuaded a Guildford tailor to place the cycle in his shop window. It soon sold and John repeated the exercise. In January 1895 he opened his own shop, the Universal Athletic Stores, at 94a High Street, which sold sports goods. Bicycles were assembled in the garden behind the shop with the cycle frames suspended from the branches of a pear tree!

John's brother, Raymond (born 1878) moved up to Guildford within months of the shop opening to become a junior partner in the business. For young people, cycling was fast becoming the 'in thing' and the business sold its Speed King and Speed Queen cycles for men and women respectively. Raymond Dennis also gave cycle lessons to those new to the 'sport' and these took place on local lanes, or if wet, in a drill hall.

In 1898, the brothers produced their first motorised vehicle – a tricycle with a single cylinder motor. John Dennis was caught speeding on this machine. He was clocked doing 16mph up the High Street which resulted in a £1 fine; but he turned this to the firm's advantage advertising the fact that his machine had both rapidity and strength while going up a steep slope. By the turn of the 20th century the brothers were also building quadricycles. These were steered by a tiller and were the forerunners of Dennis' s first motor cars.

Following a move to premises in the former militia barracks in Friary Street, Dennis's first car rolled off the production line in 1902. By then the firm had moved again to Britain's and possibly the world's first purpose-built car factory on the corner of Bridge Street and Onslow Street (see previous chapter). By now Dennis Brothers Ltd had been formed with four directors.

In those days owning a motor car was a novelty. But some impressive performances at hill climb trials and non-stop runs ensured that Dennis cars were competing with the best in Britain. Dennis's 8hp (horse-power) car

Sir Raymond Dennis KBE. (1878-1939).

the Coventry firm of White & Poppe powered it, a company Dennis later bought out. The fire engine also had a very effective Gwynne-Sergeant turbine water pump.

Following the outbreak of World War One Dennis helped the war effort by supplying 7,000 lorries to the War Office. At the height of construction, the workforce was turning out 30 lorries a week. However, production of motor cars had ceased just before the war and the firm was now concentrating wholly on commercial vehicles. These not only included a variety of buses, fire engines and lorries, but specialist vehicles such as road-sweeping machines, dust carts, cesspool-emptying vehicles and mobile canteens, to name but a few of the designs produced at the Woodbridge Hill works.

In 1916, to help combat a housing shortage in the town, Dennis built 28 houses for its employees in

cost 280 guineas, while a 10hp car was offered at 320 guineas.

A breakthrough in design came in 1903, when Dennis introduced its worm-drive rear axle. This improved its vehicles' reliability over its competitors many of whom were using a chain-driven system. To widen its sales field, commercial vehicles were added to the sales catalogue and in 1904, the first 15cwt Dennis van was sold to Harrods. Soon to follow was Dennis's first bus.

The business was growing fast, so a 10-acre site was bought at Woodbridge Hill and the first building went up in 1905. It was actually second hand and had been the Torrey-Alexander Mission Hall. It came from Brixton and was dismantled piece by piece and re-erected at Guildford. Over the next 20 years the site was developed and soon the firm was the town's major employer providing work for more than 400 people.

The first Dennis fire engine was supplied to the City of Bradford Fire Brigade in 1908. An engine made by

John Cawsey Dennis JP. (1871-1939).

Nicholas Pentreath Andrew, a director and chairman of Dennis.

Ace, Arrow, Lance and Lancet were introduced and sold to a growing customer base in Britain. By this time fire engines were being sold throughout the world, no doubt due to Raymond Dennis's 60,000-mile world tour several years previously, aimed at drumming up sales.

Changes came about in 1939 with the deaths of both John and Raymond Dennis. At the helm as the firm entered the war years were chairman Nicholas Andrew, and joint managing directors Reginald Downing and William Fish.

During World War Two Dennis turned its attention to maximum production for the war effort. The workforce increased from 1,400 to 3,000 men and women, working shifts around the clock to produce trailer pumps for fire engines, armoured vehicles, small parts for aircraft, lorries for the armed forces, bombs, and perhaps most famous of all, Churchill tanks.

The roofs of the buildings were camouflaged to hide

Dennis Bros' entry in Guildford's Jubilee Procession of 1897.

Woking Road. The engine manufacturer White & Poppe was acquired in 1919 and all its output was transferred to Guildford. Dennis purchased 21 acres of land at Guildford Park to build more homes for its employees which it named Dennisville. The roads were named after key members of the board of directors. St Johns Road and Raymond Crescent are obviously named after John and Raymond Dennis, and Pentreath Avenue is named after Nicholas Pentreath Andrew, a member of the board from the formation of the original firm in 1901. He was also chairman of Dennis for more than 30 years.

The economic depression of the 1920s saw the laying off of 140 workers, when the average pay was £4 per week. However, sales of vehicles did pick up during the inter-war years, in particular buses. Models such as the

The Dennis works at Woodbridge, beside the Guildford to Woking railway line, was a familiar landmark for many years. These fire engines were destined for the Northern Ireland Fire Authority.

the factory from enemy aircraft and the glass was removed from the skylight windows and the spaces blacked out. This resulted in very cold working conditions during the winter and all work went on under artificial light.

The 1950s and 60s were again difficult decades with strong competition from other UK vehicle manufacturers.

With the business valued at £3.4 million in 1972, and despite a battle by the board of directors, Dennis was bought out by the Hestair group. It sold the Woodbridge Hill site renting back about two thirds of it

to maintain vehicle production. The company was renamed Hestair Dennis. It mostly produced fire appliances and specialist trucks, but only about 300 vehicles a year were now made.

Slowly new markets were opened up, notably in the Middle East, and with some new designs things appeared to be improving.

Buses came back into the frame and Hestair Dennis produced its popular Dominator model in 1977. With the overseas order book looking good, the company received the Queen's Award for Export, in 1977.

In November 1988, the management team bought

The Dennis Athletic Club was a popular sports association for employees. This picture postcard was mailed from Guildford to an address in Brighton on 14 October 1907. The sender, Bob, wrote to Clara, saying: 'This is our first team taken outside the works.'

An early Dennis fire engine straight out of the factory and bound for India. Vehicles like these were ordered by countries all over the world. This one is pictured at the foot of Woodbridge Hill.

Workers came from all over Britain to work at Dennis Bros. Perhaps it was some of those from Wales who formed the Dennis Male Voice Choir. This photograph was taken in Stoke Park on 6 August 1942. Pictured, from left: John Jones, Reg Nicholson, Mr Evans, Unknown, Mr Robinson, Percy Parr, Bill Penfold, Bill Gadd, Jack Millard, Cynon Davies (conductor), Unknown, Harold Parsons, Tom Davis, Alf Stemp, Eddie Wilson, Les David, Jessie Stacey, Unknown.

All smiles. The tool-room employees at Dennis, pictured in 1957.

Aerial view of the Dennis works at Woodbridge Hill.

out Hestair Dennis renaming the Guildford operation Dennis Specialist Vehicles.

The firm was then on the move to new premises at Slyfield. The old factory was fast becoming unsuitable for modern vehicle production. It must have been a sad day for many employees still with the firm as the Woodbridge Hill site was stripped and then demolished. Fortunately, a huge archive of Dennis material that included photographs of vehicles, plans and drawings and many pictures of the works itself were saved and taken to Guildford Muniment Room. They have now been transferred to the Surrey History Centre in Woking. However, it is rumoured that not everything was kept – similar material ended up in builders' skips destined for landfill sites.

When the new factory was opened it had a workforce

The North Gate entrance of the Dennis factory.

of 317. Along with the famous Dennis fire engines, Javelin, Dominator and Falcon buses were being made. The next significant development came with the Dart –

The end of an era! It's 1986 and the demolition men have moved on to the Dennis site at Woodbridge Hill.

The new Dennis Specialist Vehicles factory at Slyfield.

a bus that has been an enormous success around the world.

With imported engines made by Cummins, the chassis are built and tested at Guildford. It is still a familiar site to see a well wrapped-up driver sitting precariously on a wooden seat exposed to the elements while test-driving a grey chassis on the roads between Slyfield and the town. These then go to a multitude of coachbuilders who complete the vehicles.

So popular are these vehicles that in 1994 a factory was built in Malaysia to assemble bus chassis.

Hestair Dennis employed the grandson, and namesake, of John Dennis as its sales manager of trucks and coaches. When he was made redundant in 1985 he set up his own firm to build and repair the bodywork for fire appliances. He began with eight other former Hestair Dennis employees and his firm is also now based at Slyfield.

Dennis's centenary was celebrated in 1995 with a special marquee at that year's Surrey County Show in

Stoke Park where former employees were invited for lunch and had plenty of opportunity to meet up with old friends and talk about the old days. The firm takes a keen interest in its own history and in May 1998 held an open day at its factory that was well attended.

Visitors had the chance to look around the workshops and to view a nostalgic gathering of old Dennis vehicles. Rides were offered in a modern fire engine or on a vintage one. Visitors could also take a short trip on a brand new air-conditioned bus or on a 1950s Dennis bus of the Aldershot & District Co. The event marked the opening of a new fabrication building and TV motoring presenter Tony Mason was the

This Dennis Falcon P3 bus was built in 1950 for the East Kent Bus Company. It was withdrawn from service in 1967 and was bought by its present owner, Norman Hamshere, in 1975 who rebuilt it to its original condition. It is seen here at Wonersh in May 2001.

Motorised chassis such as these seen outside the Dennis Specialist Vehicles factory at Slyfield are still a familiar sight being test-driven in and around Guildford.

guest of honour cutting the ribbon and declaring the building open.

The latest chapter in Dennis's history came in January 2001, and it was excellent news propelling the company to the forefront of the British transport industry. Its current parent company, Mayflower, merged with the Henlys Group to form TransBus International. The *Surrey Advertiser* reported that the deal would hopefully create 50 more jobs and would enable the firm to compete with vehicle manufacturers such as Mercedes and Renault on an international level.

Pledging to keep the Dennis name on the front of its vehicles, the chief executive of the new operation, John Smith, told the press: 'We have been here 105 years and hope to be here another 105.'

COMPTON POTTERY

ONE of the most successful ventures to revive the dying art of handicrafts among the working classes took place at a village near Guildford.

The Compton Potters' Arts Guild was the brainchild of Mary Watts, the wife of the Victorian artist George Frederick Watts.

Not only did they enlist the help of villagers to build a memorial chapel, but a pottery was established that throughout the first part of the 20th century produced a whole range of terracotta and ceramic items, many of which are now highly collectable.

George Frederick Watts (1817-1904) has been called England's Michelangelo and was a painter, sculptor and moralist of the late Victorian era. His work has been highly praised by some, but dismissed by others as downright awful!

He married his second wife, Mary Fraser-Tytler (1849-1938), in 1886, and in 1891 they came to live at the house Limnerslease, in Compton. It has been said that Watts was a hypochondriac, although he was often genuinely ill. But he liked life in rural Compton and rode a horse around the village and even taught himself to ride a bicycle.

He and his wife were dedicated supporters of a movement launched in 1885 that was known as the Home Arts and Industries Association. The thought behind it was that young artisans with little formal education could be introduced to the world of arts and crafts, leading them away from 'a life of idleness, gambling and drinking'.

Compton Pottery c.1910.

Decorative bookends made at Compton Pottery.

Classes would be held during the winter months where pupils would learn how to use their hands at a craft that would at first be a hobby, but might lead them to executing it to a professional standard.

Mary Watts had planned to start her own classes in Compton, while her husband had mind to make some

157

Watts Memorial Chapel soon after it was built in 1904.

sort of gift to the village. The solution lay in the building of a chapel.

A new burial ground was needed, as the old graveyard by the church was nearly full. In March 1895 the parish council approved a scheme whereby land that had been offered by the Loseley estate could become a cemetery. The chapel would be the gift of Watts, with his wife teaching and encouraging villagers to help create Celtic terracotta symbols and paint the intricate interior panels by an art technique known as gesso.

The project fulfilled the principals of George and Mary Watts' art movement, whereby people did something as a public service rather than for personal profit.

The Bishop of Winchester consecrated the Watts Chapel on 1 July 1898. In recent years it underwent major refurbishment. It is a wonderful building of red brick and tile, produced from local clay, and enriched with Celtic and art nouveau decorations. The Celtic-

inspired designs – Mary Watts had spent her childhood at her family's castle on the shores of Loch Ness – continued in the wares produced by the pottery.

Before work had begun on the chapel, a seam of Gault Clay had been found in the grounds of Limnerslease which provided the perfect raw material to model from. The evening classes in the village continued and the Compton Potters' Arts Guild was formed.

Initially funded by her husband, Mrs Watts' venture expanded to produce terracotta garden ornaments and gravestones. When they were exhibited at major Home Arts and Celtic Arts exhibitions in London they attracted even more buyers.

Production outgrew the manufactory at Limnerslease, so a pottery with a thatched roof was built. Next came the Watts Gallery, built as a permanent home for Watts' paintings and sculptures. Local amateur architect Christopher Turnor designed the building in the true philosophy of the Arts and Crafts

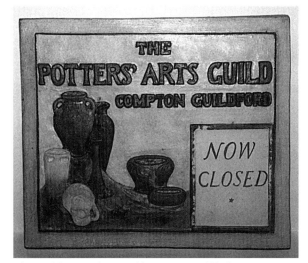

Plaque of the Potters' Arts Guild, Compton, Guildford.

movement. It also contained living accommodation for a community of young apprentice potters. The gallery was opened to the public in 1904 and is still open today and well worth a visit.

Apart from the huge terracotta urns, sundials, gravestones and other garden ornaments designed by Mrs Watts and manufactured by the workforce at the pottery, ceramic pots, vases, wall tiles, pendants, figures and even models of some Compton buildings were all made there. The pottery flourished until the 1950s and visitors to the gallery could watch the young potters at work. Many of the smaller wares were sold as souvenirs. Most were marked with the words 'Compton Pottery'. Others have a special mark containing the motto of the pottery: 'Their work was as it were a wheel in the middle of a wheel.'

After Mrs Watts' death in 1938, the guild and the pottery became a limited company run by artist George Aubertin.

Short films were often shown between television programmes in the 1950s. They were called the *Interlude*. One such film showed the hands of a potter at work. They were Aubertin's.

The smaller ceramic items made at the Compton Pottery have yet to come to the wider attention of collectors. However, examples of the larger terracotta urns and planters characterised by their Celtic designs of interwoven foliage, birds and beasts, have been offered by some of the major London auction houses and have been known to make sums in the region of four figures.

The most recent development in the story of the Watts Chapel was the major restoration work that took place in the late 1990s. Funds were raised locally in a number of ways including £4,000 from the proceeds of the Compton Pageant, which was produced by Marion and Dennis May of Shamley Green, in the summer of 1996.

Waverley Borough Council donated £1,000 to help save the unique Grade I-listed building. And, English Heritage's £121,000 from money donated by the National Lottery Fund was a huge boost and ensured the restoration work got under way.

Although the majority of the terracotta roof tiles were in good condition, an early form of concrete underneath the tiles and consisting of sulphur-rich clinker was having a devastating effect on another part of the structure. Rainwater running off was creating sulphuric acid which in turn was attacking the ironwork, which had to be replaced.

A number of tiles, however, did need replacing and they were ordered from Swallow Tiles of Cranleigh. Many craftspeople from all over the UK helped with the project and today Watts Memorial Chapel is back to its former glory on the hill a short distance from Watts Gallery itself.

FLANDERS BY MOONLIGHT – GUILDFORD IN WORLD WAR ONE

WORLD War One had dragged on for four long years and by the autumn of 1918 Britain was prepared to do anything it could to see a swift end to hostilities.

There was, however, some good news as the Allies were making considerable advances against Germany on Europe's Western Front. German moral was low and victory was in sight.

As the Germans retreated at an ever-increasing rate, Allied commanders turned their attention to the armistice demands that they would hopefully soon make. Meanwhile, the fighting went on and money was still required to 'feed the guns'.

In Guildford there had been a number of schemes to raise money for the war effort. Both the townsfolk and the business community had contributed generously but its most spectacular fund-raising enterprise came right at the end.

Just a month before men laid down their arms the town embarked on its Great Feed The Guns Effort. Its slogan was 'Buy all you can and then buy a bit more'.

However, the scheme needed a focal point or attraction to ensure the cash rolled in. Mr Fentum Phillips came up with the idea of reproducing a Western Front trench system within the town centre.

Luckily there was an area of land beside the High Street just waiting to be transformed. Three years previously a fire had destroyed the draper's store, Reeks & Co. A party of Canadian soldiers, stationed at Witley Camp, turned the site into a realistic battleground which was soon named Flanders by Moonlight. It consisted of more than 200,000 sandbags, wooden boards and other paraphernalia found in a trench system.

There was a ruined church, a large wooden cross and several dug-outs. Beneath one of them was a crypt with an improvised altar which was supposed to have replaced the one in the destroyed church. In addition there was a Red Cross dressing station with local Voluntary Aid Detachment women (VADs). Such was the realism and symbolism it couldn't fail to play on the conscience of its visitors to ensure that they dug deep into their pockets to help 'their boys' win the war and to bring them safely home.

Field telephones were rigged up and judiciously placed signs. One read: DANGER POISONED WATER, another had on it: KEEP LOW – SNIPER.

A sign by the ruined church was written in both English and French. It said: THE HIGH ALTAR IS TEMPORARILY DISMANTLED. MASS WILL BE SAID DAILY AT THE TEMPORARY ALTAR IN THE CRYPT.

Visual signals were passed from the trenches, beyond

A replica section of Western Front-style trenches opened to the public on 21 October 1918. They were constructed by Canadian soldiers on land between Guildford High Street and the Castle Grounds.

a wooden windmill, and over to the town's Castle Keep. In front of the church ruins beside a camouflaged 6in-howitzer gun Mr G.H. Brierley was waiting to stamp war certificates and bonds bought by the visitors.

The Duke of Sutherland (who lived at Sutton Place) opened the spectacle on 21 October 1918, and the crowds poured in. The fund-raising scheme ran for one week and the public were told that 15s 6d (77p) would buy 124 cartridges, £20 would buy 10 high-explosives, £100 would buy 36 three-inch shells, and £500 would buy six Vickers machine-guns; while £1,000 would buy a 20cwt three-inch anti-tank gun, ready to fire.

Guildfordians were extremely generous and at the end of the first day £90,000 had been raised. By the end of the week the grand total stood at £280,197. The final

day saw a flurry of late subscribers pledging £30,000 to ensure that the overall target was met. The town's business sector provided the majority of the overall funding, buying savings certificates or giving loans. The London City and Midland Bank pledged £30,000 alone. Motor manufacturers Dennis Bros gave £25,000, while the town's Friary Brewery contributed £10,000 with its employees adding a further £2,365.

Throughout World War One there were numerous flag days. For example, in April 1916, £425 was raised for Belgian Refugees' Day, Sick and Wounded Horses' Day in May 1917 raised £396, while the town gave £200 during Prisoners of War Day, in May 1918.

If a walk through Flanders by Moonlight, off Guildford High Street, gave a sense of what life was

Crowds begin to walk through the maze of trenches and dugouts on the opening day of Guildford's Great Feed The Guns Effort. The 'ruins of a church' can be seen in the middle foreground, the wooden cross is on the left. Beyond and to the right of the building in the centre is a wooden windmill. The Castle Keep can just be seen in the distance.

St Martha's Church covered with brush wood during the latter part of World War One thus hidden from the view of German Zeppelin pilots as they flew over Southern England.

really like in the trenches, the actual sounds of battle from far off France could, by a fluke of nature, be heard in Surrey.

The naturalist and writer Eric Parker, who lived at Feathercombe in Hambledon, was, for a time during World War One, an officer in the Queen's Royal West Surrey Regiment, guarding the gunpowder factory at Chilworth. In his book *Surrey*, published after World War Two by Robert Hale Ltd, he notes that his time spent patrolling the factory was 'two and a half years of the most monotonous work that has ever come my way'.

He relieved his boredom by observing the wildlife as he made his regular rounds. However, one day he experienced a most curious phenomenon. He had

St Martha's Church as it is today.

climbed the hill overlooking the gunpowder works to St Martha's Church and as he stood with his back to the south door of the church he could suddenly hear the war in France.

He wrote: 'Close to my ear were the sounds of battle, field guns, heavy guns, the shaking boom, the rattle of musketry, as if we were fighting Germans in the next parish. All came to me in a repercussion of sound from the oak door behind me. I stepped a yard to the side and I was in the silence of Surrey; a step to my right, and I was in France. I could be in and out of the sounds of battle as I chose, there above the Chilworth factory on a Surrey hill.'

The south door of St Martha's Church where the writer Eric Parker once heard the sounds of guns booming from France during World War One.

NORTH STREET MARKETS

FRUIT, vegetables and flowers were once the mainstay of the market stalls in North Street and many stalls were handed down from father to son. Today there are fewer than ever as shoppers are drawn to out-of-town superstores.

Guildford held its first market more than 700 years ago. Traditionally Tuesdays and Saturdays were market days and for centuries they were held in the High Street.

North Street became the preferred venue in 1865, because animal pens were restricting the movement of traffic up and down the High Street.

The market spread from North Street to adjoining

The final day of the original fruit, vegetable and flower market in North Street in 1896 before it moved to the cattle market site in Woodbridge Road.

Stalls are set up for business in North Street, c.1960. The buildings occupied by Alfred Bull Ltd, were later demolished to make way for Guildford Library.

streets such as Ward Street and Red Lion Gate, later renamed Market Street. Here and in North Street fruit and vegetables, flowers and fish were sold between 1887 and 1896. The whole market then moved to a new site off Woodbridge Road, now occupied by the police station and the law courts.

Market stalls returned to North Street on 29 August 1919. There had been severe food shortages during the latter part of World War One; German submarines were sinking many of Britain's supply ships. It was not uncommon to see lengthy queues outside food shops. Items such as margarine, butter, tea, jam and sugar were the main commodities in short supply, but meat was also scarce.

There must have been many glum faces on 7 January 1918, which was called Jointless Sunday. Families had to do without their traditional Sunday joint and make do with fish or eggs instead.

Compulsory rationing for meat, margarine and butter was introduced on 25 February that year and everyone in the borough of Guildford was issued with a ration book.

Publications were appearing that offered alternative recipes. They suggested people gather nettles and other wild plants while there was a lack of green vegetables. One book went so far as to describe ways of baking hedgehogs in clay and how to cook rats! Thankfully, the situation did not get that bad.

In Guildford, more and more land was being used for garden allotments. Even after the armistice food was still in short supply, so people were encouraged to grow their own. Some growers, who were producing more than their families' required, were able to sell their surplus for a small profit. This is when the stalls began appearing in North Street.

At the beginning of 1919 the council was still obtaining, by compulsory purchase, plots of land that could be turned over to garden allotments. On 19 May 1919, the *Surrey Times* reported that the Guildford & District Federation of Allotment Societies was suggesting that a register be drawn up of all allotmentees in order to secure an equal distribution of plots.

To tend an allotment was certainly a popular thing to do in the early summer of that year, but just how much time people were spending on their plot was soon to be questioned.

The Vicar of Stoughton, the Revd C.H.T. Ecob, held a service of blessing at the allotments tended by the Stoughton Allotment Club. With about 100 growers and their families present, he told them that although he too was an enthusiastic allotment holder he thought that growers should 'put their backs against Sunday cultivation'. There was no need to work on their plots on Sundays when they should be at church. 'God would provide,' he told them, 'if they ceased Sunday labour.'

The local newspapers were also publishing regular gardening columns that gave tips on how to grow fruit and vegetables. However, as food supplies increased, more and more people were applying for a pitch at the North Street market, but not all of them had fruit and vegetables to sell.

The council had a tricky decision to make when people who wanted to sell clothes and general household goods began applying for pitches. Some of them were from London and certain members of the council were fearful that by the sound of their names they could be 'German Jews'. Another member of the council suggested that it would be a good move to allow traders from London to set up stalls in the town as their 'cheap goods would be a benefit to Guildfordians'. The council decided that goods other than fruit, vegetables and flowers could be sold, but applicants had to live within a 10-mile radius of the borough. It was also feared that with winter coming there would soon be a shortage of fresh locally-grown produce and so the market would fizzle out unless non-food items were offered for sale.

Gradually these rules were relaxed and by the 1930s North Street on a Saturday night was alive with street traders selling all manner of goods from china, glass, clocks, watches and jewellery to second-hand items, and sweets and toys, alongside the obligatory fruit and vegetables.

They were the days of Garcia – the Chocolate King, the Fruit King, and a man called Marks who had his

North Street market before the decline in the number of fruit, vegetable and flower stalls.

Lou Lewis is a familiar face on Guildford's fruit and vegetable stalls.

pitch at the top of North Street and sold cloth and other fabrics as well as army boots. Some traders entertained the crowds with their distinctive sales patter. The Chocolate King would wrap two large bars of chocolate together and cry: 'Go on, sixpence the pair'.

In 1933, the *Surrey Weekly Press* published an article written by a person called Hamish Kirkwood, which painted an evocative picture of the Saturday night markets. It was a time when many of the shops also remained open. The headline above the article was: 'So This Is Guildford'. Part of that article is reproduced here.

It is North Street; it is Saturday night. Everyone with anything to buy or sell or say or do has elbowed his or her way to this wide thoroughfare and its usual placid aspect is lost beneath the tread of a thousand people.

People with money to spend or earn; all types are there, intermingled with the buses and the bands in the great confusion. Country folk mostly, who believe that better value can be

Looking down on to the hustle and bustle of North Street market.

obtained from a stall than from a shop and who find in the informality of the first, something more closely akin to their own make-up then in the conventionality of the second.

Stalls straggle along near the gutter. Some mere wooden counters, others more palatial and every one too small for the piled-high produce which fills it and overflows across the street. Fruit and flowers predominate, whilst here and there are stalls of sweets or meat or fish. And over all, the smell of the naphtha flares mingling with that of the fish and the flowers.

The stall-holders, too, like their wares, are contrasted. There are sons of the soil and sons of Israel haranguing the crowd. But it is the latter whose efforts are proving most lucrative. They are clever these dark-eyed curly-haired boys. Their smiles, their quips and unfailing rhetoric, draws the crowd ever nearer. Half reluctant, and not a little suspicious, their number swells gradually, whilst unceasingly the badinage continues. Never for a moment, however, do those dark eyes leave the faces before them, as they watch for that change of expression which denotes that a point has gone home. Then do they push a bag of this or that into the hands of the customer, who is too surprised to demur, and in a thrice the hard-earned money has passed from palms horny to palms not so horny. With a self-conscious, sheepish grin the purchaser then recedes to the background midst the ridicule of his friends, there to inspect, with secret anticipation, that which has been thrust upon him.

Box after box is opened. The finished boxes pile up behind the stall. In these poorly-clad children search diligently for such flotsam and jetsam as may have been left amongst the sawdust. The salesman does not mind. Nothing worth having is in those boxes now, and a reputation among the crowd for generosity is good for business.

And so it goes on. The sellers, their time now drawing quickly to an end, redouble their efforts.

Their gestures become more gesticulatory; their voices more hoarse; their descriptions more eloquent, until the common cabbage sounds like caviare, and the marrow like manna.

The shoppers, as their bags become full and their purses empty, are more querulous; more averse to the elbows and feet of their fellows. The street, near the stalls, has long since disappeared from sight beneath the paper and sawdust and rubbish. And all over still hangs the smell of naphtha flares, and the fish, and the flowers.

Suddenly the bells tolls. It is the signal that the selling must cease; that the Great God Babel's hour is at an end. Quickly the stalls are pulled down and packed into carts and motor vans. In a short space of time there is nothing left, except, of course, the paper and the rubbish.

The Saturday night market did not last and by the 1950s the Friday and Saturday daytime markets were exclusively fruit, vegetables and flowers. In 1979 the *Surrey Advertiser* reported that the winds of change were blowing through the town's famous market, and following a long battle with the borough council, the North Street Market Traders' Association had been given permission for a one-year trial period to allow traders to sell other goods.

The newspaper said that the association had claimed that many of the stallholders were finding it difficult to make ends meet – particularly those stalls at the library end of the market. It added that stallholder George Hone, 'a familiar face on the market for several years', volunteered to be the first and set up shop with toys, electrical goods and even slimming and beauty aids.

Costermongers have not only been selling their wares in North Street. At one time there was a fruit and veg stall and a flower stall at the entrance to the railway station.

The stallholders who occupied a pitch under Tunsgate were devastated when arsonists set fire to their stalls during a night-time attack in June 1994. The blaze not only destroyed the stalls but also damaged the historic arch itself. There was plenty of sympathy and good wishes from their customers and soon the

The devastated owners of the market stalls under Tunsgate Arch after vandals had set fire to the stalls in June 1994.

stallholders were back trading with mobile stalls that could be taken down at night.

Back to North Street and in 1979 there were 23 fruit stalls and six flower stalls. Many of them were local people whose families had worked the market for several generations. At the beginning of 2001 the number had fallen to five fruit stalls and three flower stalls. The current chairman of the traders' association is Phil Harrington, who has worked the market for over 50 years, since he was a boy. He has followed in the footsteps of his father and his uncles. He is one of the first to admit that it gets harder each year to make a living out of street markets.

Faces that were once familiar to thousands of Guildfordians week in, week out have now gone. In 1994, the *Surrey Advertiser* reported on John Callaghan who was giving up his plant and bulb stall after 25 years. His father had owned a stall before him, and John estimated that the Callaghans had been trading in the town for 40 years. However, he had not lived locally. Home was Bromley in Kent. He also estimated that over the years he had driven something like 175,000 miles between his home and Guildford. He said he was giving up his pitch to concentrate on expanding his landscaping business full-time.

THE 1930S WORK FUND AND THE BUILDING OF THE LIDO

T HE great depression of the 1930s left many people without work, including those in the relatively affluent south. In 1932 the Mayor of Guildford, William Harvey, launched a brilliant scheme, probably the first Britain had seen, which raised thousands of pounds and created jobs for unemployed men.

It was known as the Work Fund and Guildfordians who were earning a wage, or who were suitably well off, were asked to contribute in whatever way they could to support it.

William Harvey came from Ashford in Kent. He had been a dispatch rider during World War One and had won the Military Medal. He opened an outfitters store in Guildford in 1919. In 1926 he joined the town council. He was made Mayor in 1931 and elected for a second term the following year.

He launched the Work Fund as soon as he was re-elected as Mayor on Wednesday 9 November 1932. In reporting the event, the *Surrey Weekly Press* said it was 'probably the first scheme of its kind in the country. For that reason Guildford, and its mayor, can take pride in having set an example for other cities, municipalities and towns to emulate'.

The council had already set aside £3,000 to pay men for work that was much needed in the borough. The

William Harvey OBE, whose Work Fund raised money and helped create jobs for the unemployed in the 1930s.

SURREY   WEEKLY   PRESS.

EVERY SHILLING MEANS AN HOUR'S WORK

THE MAYOR OF GUILDFORD'S STRIKING SCHEME FOR UNEMPLOYMENT RELIEF.

Thank-Offerings from Those in Work.

EVERYONE INVITED TO HELP IN TOWN'S GESTURE.

One of the biggest problems before the country at the present time is that of unemployment, and being a national problem its ravages are also felt locally.

For some years its hideous shadow has been hanging over England like a pall, and although Guildford has been spared the extreme suffering which unemployment brings in its wake, those who pass along North Street in the vicinity of the Employment Exchange any day of the week realise that some of their fellow residents are among the unfortunates.

On Wednesday, Councillor Wm. Harvey was elected Mayor of Guildford for the second year, and he set seal to his term of office by launching a scheme for the relief of local unemployment—a scheme praiseworthy in its practicability, sound in detail, and one that will kindle anew the individual spirit in the hearts of those pressed down by absence of work.

It is probably the first scheme of its kind in the country, and for that reason Guildford, and its Mayor, can take pride in having set an example for other cities, municipalities and towns to emulate.

Newspaper cutting from the Surrey Weekly Press, 11 November 1932.

Cutting from the Surrey Weekly Press, 9 December 1932.

MAYOR'S WORK FUND.

£3,200 Subscribed; 5,000 Responses.

139 MEN AT WORK

The figures in relation to the Mayor's Work Fund Scheme up to yesterday were as follows :

Total	£3,261
Amount available for this week	£244
No. of men this week's share will employ ...	140
Responses to appeal ...	5,080
Total no. of hours worked	8,400
Total required to ensure success	£16,000
Paid in wages last week...	£162
No. of men working yesterday	139
Approximate no. of adults who have yet to respond	16,920

The latest suggestion to be made in connection with the Mayor of Guildford's work fund is that firms which have benefitted as a result of the De-rating Act should be asked to help now that the time has come when the rate could well be made use of.

Space in advertisements for fund propaganda has been offered by several firms, and also opportunities for giving explanations of the scheme in commercial magazines circulated by local firms among their own immediate and prospective customers.

Multiple Firms Helping.

Contributions are being received from the headquarters of multiple firms in respect of their establishments in Guildford, and it is hoped that managers of branch shops will co-operate by forwarding a copy of the Mayor's appeal to their head offices, together with a letter pointing out what is being done, and asking for support from their particular firm.

Applications for copies of the outline of the scheme are still pouring in from mayors, town clerks, urban and rural authorities, employment exchanges and social service organisations all over the country, and the first edition of 1,000 copies has been exhausted. A new edition is being printed, and applicants will be supplied with copies, it is hoped, by to-morrow.

Extension to New Areas.

Now that the scheme is "well under way" the Mayor has decided to approach Hambledon and Guildford Rural District Councils, with the object of including in the scheme unemployed men residing in the areas to be added to the borough on April 1st.

Longer Working Week Suggested.

A question in relation to the working hours was asked the Mayor on Wednesday by Mr. S. H. Ratcliff, a member of the Local Employment Committee, who enquired whether the 35-hour week could be extended to 40 hours. He said that men who had had a long spell of unemployment invariably were forced to "run up" debts, and immediately he resumed

Work Fund also got off to a flying start with a £100 donation from Mr H. Serpell, a former High Sheriff of Surrey.

Mr Harvey said that amounts as low as twopence in the pound earned weekly would be appreciated. The fund had a slogan: 'Every Shilling Means an Hour's Work'.

As the chief citizen, Mr Harvey added that he believed the town's unemployment figure was manageable and that Guildford's men wanted work and not charity. He called on those who had a job – and it did not matter what that job was, whether it was that of a bishop or a dustman – to assist and that their cash would be turned into work.

He believed that the greater part of the money raised would come from those who were earning between £2 and £4 per week. He said that it was because those people often knew what unemployment was like.

At that time the population of the borough was about 40,000. During October of 1932, it was recorded that there were 657 people unemployed. Britain was bracing itself for a difficult winter as the economic condition was expected to worsen.

In Guildford everything was in place for the Work Fund to begin. However, some argued that it would have been better to put up the rates and let the council employ those out of work. William Harvey disagreed, saying that an increase in the rates would have put an extra burden on the householder who was just above the poverty line – those were the people he was anxious to safeguard from greater difficulties than they were already up against.

The scheme got under way with notices in the local press and a letter was sent to every household in Guildford, delivered by unemployed auxiliary postmen. A collection box was installed inside the Guildhall where donors on a regular basis, or passers by could place contributions.

Within a week £321 6s 8d had been raised. It was announced that this figure added up to 6,426½ hours'

The caption to this Surrey Advertiser *picture read: 'Mayor of Guildford's workmanlike dive into the Stoke Park swimming pool.' The Mayor, William Harvey, had the honour of being the first into the water at the official opening on 21 June 1933.*

work. One of the first schemes was to provide work for 40 men pulling up weeds at the Sports Ground in Woodbridge Road.

It was calculated that by estimating the total number of unemployed people in the borough, each man given employment through the Work Fund would receive a minimum 35 shillings a week for about 35 hours' work.

The press reported that every shilling donated to the fund would:

- Mean an hour's work.
- Go into the pocket of an unemployed man.
- Give him the moral value of an hour's work.
- Save a similar sum in taxation and rates.
- Pay for work of importance in the town.
- Circulate right through the community.
- Help a Guildford man keep his self-respect.
- Give you the feeling that you have really helped.

It was assured that there would be no amateur recruiting or exploitation of labour and that trade union rates of pay, where they applied, would be paid.

Along with money, messages were also put in the box at the Guildhall. Wrapped around three halfpennies was a piece of paper. On it was written: 'A working man's daily bus fare'. Another note put in the box with some cash simply said: 'my mite'.

Old gold was also asked for, which could be sold to benefit the fund. Soon a gold sovereign turned up in the collection box. It too came with a note: 'From a chimney sweep, my last piece of gold'.

Local companies helped to swell the fund and so did churches, the rotary club and the Guildford branch of the Royal British Legion. There were fund-raising events that included a football match which the mayor was invited to kick off.

By the end of the first week of December work had been found for 139 men and £3,200 had been subscribed. On 23 December, the *Surrey Weekly Press* reported that 385 men were now in work and £4,221 had been raised.

The Sports Ground had been weeded – not the most interesting of tasks it has to be said – but more stimulating jobs were about to begin. These included: improvements to Allen House grounds, removing chalk

When the lido opened, outfitters and clothes shops in Guildford soon stocked the latest swimwear. These advertisements appeared in the Surrey Weekly Press on 23 June and 7 July 1933.

from the caverns at Racks Close to make them more accessible to visitors, levelling and clearing a disused tip at Mount Farm, clearing and levelling the new sports ground at the County School, planting hedges at Westborough, preparing ground for improvements at the sewage works, and perhaps the most fundamental act of employment of the whole Work Fund – helping to build the lido.

The decision to go ahead with the town's first 'open-air bathing pool, with sunbathing facilities' was made at

Plenty of picture postcards showing the lido were published in the years before World War Two.

the end of 1932. Discussion over the previous two years included reservations about its situation so near to Stoke Church. Members of the church were worried that people bathing at an outdoor pool would upset those worshipping inside the church. However, the plan was passed and building work started before the year was out. Immediately men employed through the Work Fund were using their skills alongside other contractors at the lido site.

The lido cost £13,700 to build and at its official opening on 21 June 1933, William Harvey declared it open. He was the first person to dive in and take a swim.

It was advertised that entry charges (whether bathing or not) were Sundays and weekdays (excepting Tuesday and Saturday mornings) 6d per person; Tuesdays and Saturday mornings 1 shilling, afternoons 6d. On bank holidays the entry fee rose to 9d per person, children 4d.

A monthly adult season ticket cost 7s 6d. 'Light flimsy costumes' were banned and the car park was free except on gala days.

When the Work Fund closed in 1933, some £10,000 had been raised and more than 150,000 hours of work had been provided.

In the 1934 New Year Honours List William Harvey was appointed OBE. He was also rewarded with the honorary freedom of the borough of Guildford. It was said that his Work Fund scheme had been mentioned in more than 100 British provincial newspapers. There had been many inquiries from other towns and cities, not only in Britain, but also in France, Germany and the USA.

To quote the saying of the time, it certainly was 'money for work done' and not 'money received for no work done'.

BUY A BRICK FOR THE CATHEDRAL

I T WAS 1954 and the building of Guildford Cathedral had all but come to a standstill. It took the then Mayor of Guildford, Leslie Codd, who freely admitted that he was not a churchgoer, to get the project moving again after criticising those in the Church for not doing enough to generate funds. He was responding to an outburst by the Provost of Holy Trinity Church, Walter Boulton, who had attacked the town council and the public over its apathy towards the unfinished cathedral.

A turning point in the resumption of the building of the Cathedral of the Holy Spirit on Stag Hill was on Wednesday 24 November 1954, at a conference held by the Diocese of Guildford in Woking. Leslie Codd took many of the clergy gathered there by surprise with the words: 'The unfinished building is a discredit to Guildford. You have either to sell the Cathedral or build it.' His suggestion was to raise the profile of the buy a brick campaign with the slogan: 'Give the Cathedral a gift for Christmas'. What better way, he asked, was there to celebrate the birth of Christ?

Guildford Cathedral is only the second Anglican cathedral in the UK to be built on an entirely new site since Salisbury Cathedral was begun in 1220. The other is Liverpool Cathedral.

Leslie Codd whose rallying speech in 1954 helped to re-start efforts to complete the building of Guildford Cathedral.

With the creation of the Diocese of Guildford in 1927, it was soon realised that the building which became the Cathedral Church, Holy Trinity, in the High Street, would not be big enough and could not be enlarged. In 1928 plans were announced for the building of a new cathedral. A perfect east west aligned location on top of Stag Hill covering some six acres was donated by the Earl of Onslow. It was close enough to the town centre and afforded an excellent high position so that the building could be seen for miles around.

An open competition in 1932 saw designs submitted by 183 architects. The winner was Edward Maufe with a design incorporating red bricks and limestone. The first sign that building work was about to begin on Stag Hill was the erection of a lofty teak cross made of timbers from the battleship *HMS Ganges*. This was in April 1933 and with the country entering a period of economic depression, some may have wondered if the project would ever get off the ground.

The Archbishop of Canterbury, Dr Cosmo Gordon Lang, laid the foundation stone on 22 July 1936, and soon after the first of 778 concrete piles was driven into hill. Older residents will recall that the work went on day and night and literally shook the town.

Each pile weighed about five tons and between 1,200 and 1,500 blows was

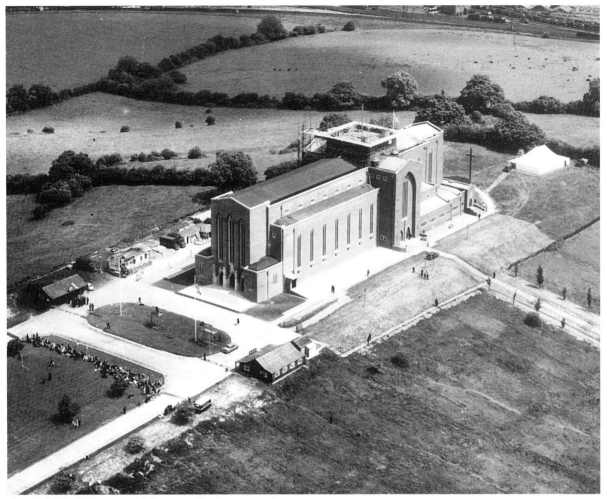

Guildford Cathedral in 1961, with the tower still to be constructed.

needed by the four-ton steam hammer to drive them to the correct depth. Queen Mary was present when the final one was driven in and the town then received some much-needed peace and quiet. On 25 May 1938, the first brick was cemented into place by the then Mayor of Guildford, Harold Gammon.

All construction work stopped when World War Two began in September 1939. There was, however, some necessary work undertaken to protect unfinished wall heads from the rain, but large parts of the building were completely exposed to the elements.

Fears that it would become a target for enemy aircraft proved unfounded. Although an anti-aircraft gun was placed near Stag Hill, the nearest bombs that

fell were just to the south at Onslow Village. Some believed that the Luftwaffe spared the Cathedral as it was a useful navigation aid.

The Guildhall clock, which had been removed from its position over the High Street for safe keeping, was stored in the crypt of the Cathedral during the war years.

In 1948 building work resumed. Many windows were glazed, including three stained glass windows. The transept roof was added and the base of the tower was constructed. Plastering was completed, heating pipes installed and the floor of the choir and the sanctuary finished before work slowed to a trickle.

Enter the local Labour politician Leslie Codd, who

Architect Sir Edward Maufe's dramatic sketch showing how the first part of Guildford Cathedral would look. It was published in the Surrey Advertiser *on 18 July 1936, shortly before the foundation stone was laid.*

had come to Guildford from Manchester and was in charge of the publicity department for the Guildford & District Co-operative Society.

Although great sums of money had already been raised, Codd was not pleased with the Cathedral's situation. In September 1954 he had written to the press informing them of the newly formed Mayor of Guildford's Cathedral Fund. In it he said the immediate object was assisting towards the building of a substantial part of the nave by 1956 and subsequently the completion of the building as a whole. The letter was signed by no less than eight previous Guildford mayors.

Two months later he told the

diocese conference: 'What worries me is the lack of a sense of urgency on the part of all you churchpeople with regard to getting in funds immediately.' He went on to warn them that they had either had to build it, or sell it – to become something like a furniture depository.

'It looks like a blessed factory,' he told the clergy

The brick signed by Queen Elizabeth II when she visited Guildford Cathedral in 1957.

gathered at the conference, 'but inside it is one of the most beautiful things I have ever seen.'

He went on to tell them: 'You can't spread the Word today without hard cash. As a business investment it is very important to build the Cathedral.' He added that if it were built there would be a tremendous increase in the number of people joining the Church.

His words were indeed a turning point. The Bishop of Guildford, Dr Montgomery Campbell, spoke about lack of unity in the diocese and urged anyone who opposed the building to come out in the open and give his or her reasons.

The idea of selling bricks for the Cathedral had been suggested before the war by the architect's wife, Prudence Maufe. However, the idea had not been taken up. Now it appeared to strike a chord with people in the awareness to raise funds. It certainly helped to raise the profile of Guildford Cathedral throughout the world. Bricks and brick tokens were purchased and other donations and gifts poured in.

The brick tokens were sold for 2s 6d (12½p) and the campaign went on into the 1960s until the Cathedral was consecrated in May 1961.

Bricks could be bought at the Cathedral itself and books of brick tokens were distributed to fundraisers far and wide. One visitor to the Cathedral who was asked whether he would like to buy a brick, jokingly replied: 'What flavour are they – strawberry or vanilla?' In those days ice cream wafers were sold as 'bricks'.

Everyone who bought a brick could sign his or her name on it. The Queen and Prince Philip visited the Cathedral in 1957 and their signed bricks are on display.

At the end of 1960 there was a ceremony at the Cathedral attended by Leslie Codd when a box containing stubs from the brick tokens was sealed into a niche near the entrance to the nave. The stubs contain the names of those who bought brick tokens.

Mr Codd said: 'It is given to few men in connection with such a great project to see their dream come true within their own lifetime, let alone the remarkably short period of five years.'

He also paid tribute to Eleanora Iredale, who was the

Poster promoting the Buy a Brick campaign illustrated by the artist E.H. Shepard.

secretary of the New Cathedral Fund. When she retired from the post in 1962 she had been responsible for raising in the region of £660,000 for the building, over a period of 11 years. This story would not be complete without mentioning her tremendous work.

Not only did she organise fund-raising schemes but she regularly scanned the columns of the financial press to monitor the fortunes of companies whose materials were being used in the Cathedral's construction. If, for example, a company was showing healthy profits, she would contact its directors and cajole them into providing additional materials free of charge!

In the region of £50,000 was raised through the sale of bricks, but the sale of brick tokens was not so

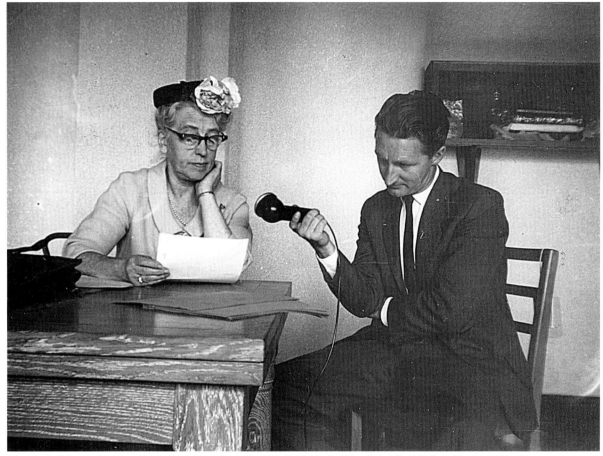

Eleanora Iredale, seen here recording an interview, helped raise £660,000 for the building of Guildford Cathedral between 1952-62.

successful. A report in 1962 stated that out of 10,000 brick books originally printed, 8,983 were not issued or returned unused. The amount raised was £6,000.

However, the auditors added that this state of affairs was not unusual and there was certainly no money outstanding, dishonesty or misappropriation of funds.

The notion of the brick fund itself and the stern words of Leslie Codd without doubt kick-started the final push to complete our cathedral, helped by the work of Eleanora Iredale and many others who became inspired by the project in the mid 1950s.

In May 2001, to mark the 40th anniversary of the consecration of Guildford Cathedral, a brick-givers service was held along with other special events. Anyone who had bought a brick was welcome to attend.

GHOSTLY GOINGS ON

Strange happenings at the Angel Hotel and at Bushy Hill

LIKE many historic towns, Guildford can lay claim to a number of ghost stories. They range from rather puzzling mysteries to one, at least, that borders on the terrifying.

Perhaps the best known Guildford ghost story is the man in military uniform that appeared in a mirror at the Angel Hotel. Over the weekend of 30 and 31 January 1970, Mr and Mrs Dell of London were staying at the hotel. They had been given Room One – the Prince Imperial of France Room on the first floor over-looking the High Street. After dinner, the couple retired to their room for the night.

The heavily-beamed room contained a very large wardrobe with a 7ft x 4ft mirror in its centre. Mr Dell had trouble sleeping and at about 3am got out of bed and sat for a while in one of the armchairs. Several minutes later he returned to bed and as he stood up he glanced towards the mirror. There, to his great surprise, was a man's face looking back at him with a very compelling expression in his eyes. 'Am I dreaming?' Mr Dell thought to himself. He looked again and the reflection of the man was still there.

Mr Dell woke his wife and quietly beckoned to her to come and look at the mirror. For a few minutes she could not see the apparition, but then it appeared to her too. It remained for at least 30 minutes before it faded away. During that time it did not move at all. Mr Dell picked up a ball point pen and sketched what he saw on a red paper napkin.

Mr G. Dell's sketch of the ghost he saw in a mirror at the Angel Hotel in 1970.

The figure appeared to be of a moustached middle-aged man wearing a foreign-looking military uniform dating from the late 19th century.

At dinner the following evening in the Crypt

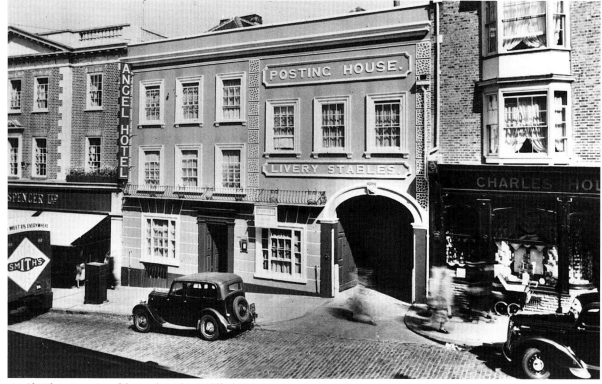

A mid 20th-century view of the Angel Hotel in Guildford High Street.

restaurant Mr Dell described what he had seen to the hotel manager Mr Kiersz. The story soon spread and was reported in the *Surrey Advertiser*. Then further stories of haunting and strange happenings at the Angel emerged.

The assistant manager, Colin Anderson, also claimed to have seen the ghost, and Mr Kiersz recalled a disturbing incident only two months earlier, also in Room One.

At about 8pm one evening the telephone switchboard flashed from the extension in Room One. When the receptionist did not get a reply from the female guest who occupied it, she made her way up to the room and knocked on the door. Again there was no reply. However, the door was unlocked. She opened it and to her surprise standing absolutely petrified in the middle of the room was the guest. She said that she had been aware of a presence and wished to be moved to another room.

The actor Roger Moore was the next person to be spooked at the Angel. According to a national newspaper he was staying there sometime in 1973 and was visited two nights running by the apparition of a man. He later told the newspaper: 'I was sitting bolt upright in my bed and watching a white ghostly figure moving towards me.

'I was frozen. I wanted to call out and scream, but couldn't. I was numb – paralysed from head to toe.

'There was a head, body and legs – but it was mist-like. I pulled myself together, somehow calmed myself and then tried to communicate with the ghost. 'I said softly, "what do you want? Are you troubled?" As I went to move from the bed, the ghost just vanished.'

Roger Moore recalled that the next night at exactly the same time, about 2am, it returned. He said: 'I thought, "It's after me. What does it want with me?"'

When he went to his room on the third night he found a Bible beside the bed opened at the *23rd Psalm, The Lord is My Shepherd*. The night passed without incident. Next morning the room maid asked casually:

Picture postcard of the interior of the Angel Hotel in about 1918. It is a building in which several unexplained events have occurred.

'Did you see the ghost last night, sir?' Roger Moore was somewhat taken aback that she knew of it and replied that he had not. She then added that she didn't think he would have been troubled.

The newspaper tracked down a former maid at the hotel who explained that several of the staff, herself included, had seen the ghost. She said the secret was to leave a Bible open at the *23rd Psalm* and the ghost wouldn't appear.

Moving on to 1985, and a member of staff at the Angel reported hearing ghostly voices just a few days before Hallowe'en.

At about 9.30pm part-time waitress Mary Dibley was walking along a corridor when she heard a voice call out to her. When she turned around there was no one there. Then, as she made her way past the laundry room and a bedroom, a woman's voice called out 'Mary'. Again she looked but there was no one there.

She checked all the nearby rooms but no one could be found. By this time she began to feel scared. She told the *Surrey Advertiser*: 'I could hear my heart thumping – it was awful. It was a sort of inquiring voice, as if there was going to be a question coming after it.'

Ghosts are not exclusive to old buildings and it is strange that the 1970s seem to have been a particularly prolific time for supernatural happenings, Guildford included.

An isolated incident was the ghost of what appeared to be a farm worker from years gone by who surprised a woman in Worplesdon one afternoon by walking right through her garden. A ghost of a woman has also been seen walking along a footpath deep within Whitmoor Common.

Arguably Guildford's most disturbing ghost story concerns a family from Merrow who were subject to an uneasy presence in their council house. This activity

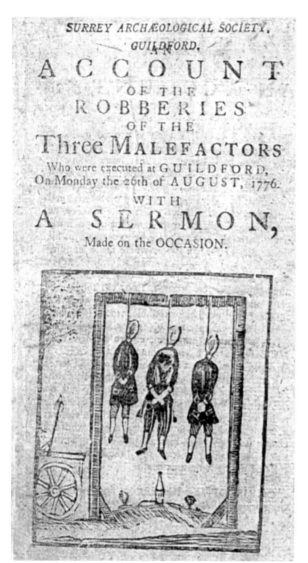

The front page of a leaflet describing the execution of three men on Ganghill Common in 1776. Merrow Church can also be seen in the illustration.

culminated in 1977 when they could not tolerate it any longer and demanded to be re-housed.

At the time of the disturbances James and Winifred Fairweather, who lived in Bushy Hill with their daughter Denise, her husband Leslie Hoare, and their two children, did not know that 200 years previously a gallows had stood there.

A pamphlet belonging to the Surrey Archaeological Society gives a fascinating account of a public execution on 26 August 1776, of James Potter, Frederick William Gregg, and Christopher Ellis. It contains an illustration of the three men on the gallows with Merrow church in the distance.

Potter was a highwayman who robbed William Calvet of 11 guineas and his watch on Banstead Downs. Ellis was a burglar and Gregg had been convicted of robbery with violence. It is recorded that at his execution Gregg 'begged all young men to avoid bad women that had brought him to this shameful death'.

Was it the ghost of one of these three men who had returned to inflict such terror on an unsuspecting family?

Over the years odd things had happened to the Fairweathers as they raised their four children in the 1950s-built three-bedroomed semi.

Mrs Fairweather once felt as if she was being pinned down in her bed by something which also made the room go cold. One of her sons was the first to see the spectre and described it as a man in an ancient costume with a long cloak and a black hat.

Birds gathered and nested in the rafters of their home. One flock actually lived in the roof space. Visits by two priests, a psychic investigator and an exorcism failed to rid them of the ghostly goings-on and from about 1969 onwards, things steadily got worse.

Then came a night in late May 1977, soon after the arrival of Denise and Leslie's second son Kevin, that the family would never forget. There was a terrific thunderstorm and the eldest son Jamie, aged two-and-a-half, was reluctant to go to bed. Eventually he was put upstairs but later woke screaming: 'That's not my daddy, take him away.' Of all the strange unexplained happenings this was the final straw. The whole family spent the night huddled together in the living room. The next day they called the police and soon the borough council granted them their wishes and rehoused the family.

BIBLIOGRAPHY

Alexander, Matthew *Guildford As It Was* Hendon Publishing Co, 1978.

Alexander, Matthew *Tales of Old Surrey* Countryside Books, 1985.

Alexander, Matthew *The Guildford Guildhall A Guide* Guildford Borough Council, 1988.

Beswick, M. *Brickmaking in Sussex: A History and Gazetteer* Middleton Press, 1993.

Brown, Stuart J. *Dennis 100 Years of Innovation* Ian Allen Publishing, 1995.

Askey, Derek *Stoneware Bottles, From Bellarmines to Ginger Beers, 1500-1949* BBR Publishing, 1998.

Chamberlin, E.R. *Guildford: A Biography* Macmillan & Co Ltd, 1970.

Cohen, Morton N. *Lewis Carroll – A Biography* Macmillan, 1995.

Collyer, Graham and David Rose *Images of Guildford* The Breedon Book Publishing Company, Derby, 1998.

Collyer, Graham and David Rose *Guildford The War Years 1939-45* The Breedon Book Publishing Company, Derby, 1999.

Corke, Shirley *Lewis Carroll in Guildford* Guildford Borough Council, 1989.

Corke, Shirley *Guildford: A Pictorial History* Phillimore & Co, Chichester, 1990.

Goodwin, John *Military Signals from the South Coast* Middleton Press, 2000.

Gould, Veronica Franklin *Watts Chapel* self published with Watts Gallery.

Janaway, John *Guildford A Photographic Record* Ammonite Books, Godalming, 1990.

Janaway, John *Surrey: A County History* Countryside Books, 1994.

Judges, E.A. *In And Around Guildford* Surrey Times, 1895.

Mitchell, Vic and Keith Smith *Southern Main Lines, Woking to Portsmouth* Middleton Press, 1985.

Morgan, Gavin *The Guildford Guy Riots* Northside Books, 1992.

Oakley, W.H. *Guildford In The Great War* Billing & Sons Ltd, Guildford, 1934.

Parker, Eric *Highways & Byways in Surrey* Macmillan & Co Ltd, 1921 edition.

Parker, Eric *The County Books Series, Surrey* Robert Hale Ltd, London.

Parker, Eric *The History of Cricket* The Lonsdale Library of Sports, Games and Pastimes, Seeley Service & Co Ltd.

Rose, David *Memory Lane Guildford & District* The Breedon Book Publishing Company, 2000.

Spring, Laurence *The Archives of Dennis Specialist Vehicles* Surrey Record Office, 1995.

Sturley, Mark *The Breweries and Public Houses of Guildford* Charles W. Traylen, Guildford, 1990.

Twelvetrees, Richard and Pepys Squire *Why Dennis and How* Guildford, 1945.

Vine, P.A.L. *London's Lost Route to the Sea* David & Charles, 1965.

Vine, P.A.L. *Surrey Waterways* Middleton Press 1987.

Williamson, Dr G.C. *The Guild Hall of Guildford and Its Treasures* 1928.

Woodforde, John *Bricks to Build a House* Routledge and Keegan Paul, 1976.

Southern Region VBS report on The Tread Wheel Crane, Guildford. 1999.

Information sheets on the history of the Wey Navigations. (National Trust, Dapdune Wharf, Guildford, 2001).

Kelly's Directories of Guildford and Godalming (various editions).

The Making of Guildford Blue (booklet to accompany working display of the manufacture of blue cloth in 1977).

Back copies of the *Surrey Advertiser*, *Surrey Times* and the *Surrey Weekly Press*.

INDEX